Declutter Mastery for Adults with ADHD

Get it Done, will you?

Boost Your Focus & Enhance Decision-Making in Just 15 Minutes with Task Chunking

I dedicate this book to my wonderful son,
Nicholas. May his Dreams come true, and his
path be filled with adventure and joy.

TESS.
R

Do Check out my author Page on Amazon.com at
https://amazon.com/author/myworkingmemoryiscrap

Contents

Chapter 13: The Fun Part!

Reasons to do this, plus a Dash of Humor; some things might make you laugh aloud!

It includes many Tales, Tips, Hacks, Excuses, why don't you keep it going, and more. So check it out, as you may see some familiar behavior patterns!

Chapter 14 Cleaning Hacks!

Introduction

Let us imagine you walk into a room in your home where every surface is covered; there are forgotten items, Newspapers, and coffee cups; it is a mess with unfinished tasks everywhere; it is a sea of clutter. For adults with ADHD, this signifies mental disarray; it encompasses more than mere tidiness. It can hinder focus and reduce effectiveness and efficiency. Research indicates that clutter raises stress and anxiety, particularly for individuals with ADHD. It intensifies symptoms and affects the quality of life. Addressing clutter is not just about making a space look neat. It is a crucial step toward improved mental health and well-being. It is essential to get your house in order figuratively, as a happy house reflects a happy mind.

I know this all too well. My brother, who is Neurodivergent and lives with Autism plus ADHD, struggles with clutter daily. Watching him spend more time searching for things than enjoying life, especially as he reaches retirement age, has been eye-opening. Our mother was much the same—an actual clutter bug. Growing up, I saw how clutter affected our family dynamics. These firsthand experiences have motivated me to write this book.

The primary goal of this book is to offer practical, ADHD-friendly solutions for decluttering. It will focus on short bursts of activity—15 minutes to be precise, daily—to keep your home tidy. This approach prevents overwhelm and allows creativity to flow. Whether tackling regular chores or organizing a single drawer, the emphasis is on short, manageable sessions that fit into busy lives. You will discover various methods to maintain a clutter-free home.

So, what can you expect from this book, a blueprint for an easy 15 minutes? It will demonstrate how it is possible to do just 15 minutes daily to gain improved organizational skills, enhanced focus, better decision-making, and a more peaceful, calm living environment. These improvements can lead to greater happiness and overall well-being. "The happiness of less" is a concept you will, I hope, come to appreciate. This book stands apart from other decluttering guides by offering ADHD-specific strategies focusing on short, effective bursts consisting of 15 minutes of daily activity.

It will also incorporate principles of mindfulness and minimalism. No self-respecting declutter guide can ignore these two critical areas.

This book will be your **go-to** reference guide for handling clutter. It will offer practical ways to approach, contain, and manage clutter as it emerges to nip it in the bud. Let us look at how the book is structured. It begins by describing the complex relationship between clutter and ADHD. This understanding is the crux of the entire book! For sure, there is clutter when ADHD is present in a relationship! Then, this book will transition to the subtle art of the many varied techniques of the practical side of decluttering per se. Finally, I will focus on how to maintain a clutter-free life. Each chapter is designed to build on the last, providing you with a clear path as we advance.

I invite you to engage in this journey actively. You could use a journal to take notes, reflect on your progress, and apply strategies to your life. You will find interactive elements and tools throughout the book to support your journey. This is not a one-time-read book but a reference—it is a blueprint for living your life without clutter to dip into as and when needed.

As I close this introduction, I will leave you with a motivational note: Imagine a life where clutter no longer holds you back. A serene, clutter-free space is within your reach. Believe in your ability to make lasting changes. Embrace this journey with an open heart and an open mind. You and you alone possess the ability to alter your environment and improve your life. Let us start.

Chapter 1: Understanding ADHD and Clutter

Why Clutter Happens, Emotional and Practical Causes of Chaos, and The Myths

When you walk into a cluttered room, you might immediately feel overwhelmed by a mountain of chaos. For many, this clutter is merely an inconvenience, but for adults with ADHD, it can become an insurmountable obstacle. The room does not just contain a physical mess; it reflects an internal struggle. It is a mirror of the mind, where thoughts and tasks can spiral out of control, leading to increased anxiety and stress. This chapter will explore why clutter is such a pervasive issue for individuals with ADHD and how understanding this connection is critical in managing the clutter, its emotional hold, and its weight.

1.1 ADHD and the Clutter Connection

Attention deficit hyperactivity disorder (ADHD) influences how individuals process information and manage tasks. Characteristics such as inattention, impulsivity, and challenges with executive function are significant contributors to clutter accumulation. For example, an individual may intend to organize their workspace but become distracted by other tasks, leading to forgotten chores and an accumulation of unfinished activities. Impulsivity adds another dimension, where spontaneous purchases contribute to clutter without a planned use.

An anecdotal instance highlights this issue: three "one pot" cooking pots were discovered in a third bedroom, although only one was necessary. The presence of two additional pots raises questions about impulsive behavior and decision-making post-surgery, particularly following brain surgery for a tumor. It is documented that brain injuries can have substantial effects on cognitive processes. This experience suggests the surgery might have influenced ADHD-like symptoms, or perhaps pre-existing symptoms were exacerbated.

Research indicates that ADHD primarily involves the frontal lobe of the brain, which regulates attention, language, social skills, impulse control, judgment, and problem-solving. However, emerging findings propose a more global perspective of the disorder, suggesting it involves broader brain networks beyond the traditionally localized regions. Evidence also supports the notion that ADHD has a substantial genetic component.

Anyway, I only know that my working memory is not what it was! Also, I can be scatty, to say the least, and I do recognize having many recognizable ADHD traits. In the words of Carlos Wallace, "You own your feelings. You own your thoughts. You control both. No one has the right to any of it—to any of you without your permission."

— Carlos Wallace, The Other 99 T.Y.M.E.S: Train Your Mind to Enjoy Serenity

With Adult ADHD, you may have issues with the following:

- Concentration
- Following directions
- Remembering information
- Organizing tasks
- Procrastination

- Boredom

- Anxiety

- Depression

- Controlling emotions can be heightened too, whereby emotions are on high alert; women particularly can burst out crying at the slightest thing.

Individuals with Rejection Sensitivity Dysphoria (RSD) and ADHD may face difficulties in handling rejection. They often report their emotions as intense or overwhelming. This condition can result in significant apprehension regarding rejection.

- Impulsiveness

- Low self-esteem

- Mood swings

- Relationship problems

- Substance abuse or addiction

- Motivation

- Restlessness

- Talking too much

- Talking out of turn

No two people with ADHD are alike. Some people look for stimulation, but others avoid it. Plus, some adults with ADHD can be antisocial & self-isolating. Others can be very social and go from one relationship to the next.

Complications of Adult ADHD

If you have adult ADHD, you could have a long-term pattern of issues in many parts of your life. This may include **School/College**

- A history of bad grades or repeating.
- Getting in trouble at school

Problems at work

- Frequent job changes
- Poor work performance
- Unhappiness with your job

Problems in life

- Speeding tickets, vehicle accidents, or having your license suspended
- Smoking or using alcohol or drugs
- Debt, gambling, or other money issues.

Overeating, including impulsively consuming unhealthy foods, can lead to various health issues.

- Impulse shopping, buying duplicates

Relationship problems

- Unstable relationships
- A history of separation or divorce
- Multiple marriages

Adult ADHD is a brain disorder affecting cognitive and executive functions, leading to impulsivity and high energy. There are three types:

- Inattentive ADHD: Characterized by disorganization, distraction, and difficulty following instructions.

- Hyperactive/Impulsive ADHD: Involves restlessness, excessive talking, and impatience.
- Combined ADHD: A mix of inattentive and hyperactive/impulsive traits.

About 4% to 5% of U.S. adults have ADHD.

Every US adult who has ADHD certainly had it as a child. Some were diagnosed in childhood, but others only found out later in life, and these account for around 60%, which is shocking that 60% did not know until Adulthood.

These difficulties with executive functions make it challenging to develop and follow an organized system, as the cognitive processes required to plan, initiate, and persist in tasks become disrupted.

Clutter, in turn, exacerbates ADHD symptoms, creating a vicious cycle of disorganization and stress. You may find yourself unable to focus amidst the chaos, leading to heightened anxiety and feelings of being overwhelmed. Simple tasks, such as finding a specific document or clothing item, can become extreme "treasure hunts" as each one drains your energy and time. A cluttered environment reduces productivity and delays every action by the need to sift through the mess, increasing time and effort. This environment can also impact self-esteem, as the inability to maintain order may feel like a personal failing rather than a symptom of ADHD.

Common clutter patterns among those with ADHD include disarrayed workspaces and overflowing closets. A desk cluttered with papers, pens, and gadgets can make concentrating on a task impossible. Closets brimming with clothes you do not wear and items you do not use can also create a sense of chaos that extends into daily life. These hotspots are not just physical spaces but manifestations of mental

clutter. The more disordered your environment becomes, the more it reflects and reinforces the internal chaos of an ADHD mind.

Clutter acts both as a symptom and a cause of ADHD experience. It is a visible manifestation of the internal disorder, where forgotten tasks and impulsive decisions accumulate in physical form. Yet, it also perpetuates the cycle, as the clutter aggravates your symptoms, making it harder to break free. Understanding this dual role is crucial. Recognizing that clutter is not simply a personal shortcoming, but a part of the ADHD experience can be liberating. It allows you to approach decluttering not just as a physical task but as a holistic practice that involves both mind and environment.

Reflection: Clutter and You

Please take a moment to reflect on your relationship with Clutter. What are the typical clutter hotspots in your home? How do these spaces make you feel, and how do they impact your ability to focus and function? Write down your thoughts in a journal. Consider the slight changes you might make to begin addressing clutter. Remember, understanding the problem is the first step toward finding a solution. Acknowledge that dealing with clutter is not about perfection but progress and creating a space supporting your well-being.

1.2 Cognitive Overload and Clutter Chaos

Cognitive overload is a formidable adversary in the life of an adult with ADHD, especially when it comes to managing clutter. Imagine juggling multiple tasks at once—preparing dinner, answering emails, and keeping track of a child's homework—only to find that the mental load paralyzes you. I often returned home from primary school and saw my mother still in bed, as though she was burying her head in the bed instead of sand! This is a common experience for individuals with ADHD, where the brain struggles to process and prioritize information effectively. An overwhelming number of tasks can lead to multitasking failures, resulting in many unfinished projects and an ever-growing clutter. This chaos is further compounded by sensory overload; the brain becomes overwhelmed by the sheer volume of stimuli presented by a cluttered environment. Visual noise can make it difficult to focus on a single task, leading to a cycle of frustration and inaction. The paralysis of choice further complicates matters, as deciding where to begin decluttering can feel insurmountable. Each decision requires mental energy, which can quickly deplete already limited cognitive resources.

Adults with ADHD face quite specific cognitive challenges that hinder decluttering efforts. Working memory deficits make it easy to forget planned decluttering sessions, while attention deficits make it difficult to focus on a single task. This reduced ability to focus and working memory deficits often result in a scattered approach, hit-and-miss, where efforts are too thin to be effective. Prioritizing tasks becomes a Herculean effort, with cluttered environments only exacerbating the confusion. For example, cleaning out a closet may seem straightforward, but the myriads of decisions about what to keep or discard can quickly become overwhelming. The result is often avoided, as the mental effort required feels too great. Suppose a veritable treasure hunt is needed whenever an item is wanted and subsequently hunted for. In that case, it quickly becomes overwhelming and is often set aside for some other, indefinite time. This avoidance can lead to a cycle where tasks build up, creating an even more significant barrier to engagement. The clutter is perceived not just as disorganization but as an essential emotional hurdle, fueling feelings of anxiety and paralysis. Each delayed attempt to find or organize something can reinforce the sense that tackling the mess is a monumental challenge, something to be avoided rather than confronted.

It is essential to recognize that this avoidance is a natural response to the stress that clutter can create. However, addressing it in small, manageable steps can shift the experience from dread to a path of empowerment. By breaking tasks into short bursts, you can integrate changes into your daily routine, turning those overwhelming challenges into achievable goals.

To avoid overwhelming feelings, it is imperative to address clutter in a manageable and non-intimidating way. By breaking down the process into short, focused sessions, individuals can gradually transform their spaces without the burden of overwhelm. Implementing consistency, minor changes can make a significant difference over time, helping to build confidence and reduce anxiety. It is about creating systems that work for you, so organizing becomes less of a daunting chore and more of a rewarding practice. This approach not only helps to declutter but also fosters a sense of control and accomplishment, paving the way for a more peaceful and efficient environment. to use practical strategies to reduce the mental burden and manage clutter effectively.

For instance, implementing simple sorting systems can provide immediate relief by creating order out of chaos. Labeling bins for donations, recycling, and items to keep can streamline the decision-making process and make the task more manageable. Digital tools also offer a lifeline, helping to track tasks and set reminders. Apps designed for organizations can simplify the process, allowing individuals to break down tasks into smaller, less daunting steps. With these tools, the brain has more space to focus on the task rather than being bogged down by endless possibilities.

Consider the daily challenges faced by individuals with ADHD in managing clutter. Balancing work commitments, household responsibilities, and personal life can seem impossible. The kitchen counter might be filled with unpaid bills, grocery lists, and children's drawings, each adding to the cognitive load. In the living room, piles of laundry and forgotten projects create a sense of chaos, making relaxation difficult. This constant state of being overwhelmed can lead to avoidance behavior, where tasks are put off to another day, the never-never pile, corner, or even spare bedroom, just because they feel too overwhelmed to tackle. While mundane, household chores can become monumental when compounded with the mental fatigue accompanying cognitive overload. The key to overcoming these challenges lies in recognizing how ADHD affects one's ability to organize and develop personalized systems that cater to those needs.

By understanding these cognitive hurdles, you can see clutter not as a personal failing but due to how your brain processes information. This realization is the first step in developing strategies aligning with your cognitive strengths and limitations, allowing you to create a more harmonious and manageable living environment.

1.3 Emotional Attachment and Sentimental Clutter

In the sphere of decluttering, emotional attachment to items poses a unique challenge, especially for those grappling with ADHD. Personal belongings often carry more than just functional value; they hold memories and stories. A simple photo album can transport you back to childhood summers, while an old sweater might remind you of someone cherished. These associations make "letting go" a formidable task that is much more difficult. For adults with ADHD, the emotional ties can feel even more substantial, as tangible items often serve as anchors in a world that sometimes feels chaotic and overwhelming. The fear of losing these connections is powerful, rooted in the belief that discarding items equates to discarding parts of one's identity.

Guilt and anxiety further complicate the process of letting go. There is often a lingering sense of guilt over wastefulness, questioning whether discarding an item is a loss of potential value. You might hold onto things with the thought, "What if I need this later?" This anxiety about future needs keeps many items from the past tightly in your grasp, cluttering not just your space but your mental landscape as well. The concern extends beyond mere practicality; it is intertwined with a more profound sense of loss. What if letting go erases a memory or severs a connection to a part of life that was once significant? These thoughts can paralyze efforts to declutter, making each decision feel fraught with consequences. I watched several family members explicitly avoid decluttering so-called items that they felt were too precious to let go as that would imply the loss of the cherished memory associated with the now defunct not working clock that was given to my brother as a gift one Christmas many years back literally over 20 years if not more. My brother retained a firm grip on items that were no longer functional or did not fit him. Having reached the age of sixty-seven and retired, he was now significantly more significant than in his youth.

Addressing emotional attachment requires gentle strategies that respect these feelings while encouraging progress. Mindful reflection exercises can provide a way forward. Taking time to review each item, noting its significance, and documenting this in a journal for its role in your life can assist with the emotional process required to move on. This practice helps reframe the act of letting go, not as a loss but as a transition to another phase in your life. Creating a memory box for cherished items can also be effective. You can preserve memories without allowing them to overrun your living space by designating a special place for the most meaningful belongings. This approach helps distinguish between what holds sentimental value and what can be released.

Consider the experience of individuals who have successfully navigated the emotional terrain of decluttering. One person found liberation in realizing that memories reside in the mind and heart, not just objects. They began by tackling their most cluttered space, acknowledging each item's emotional weight. They discovered a newfound sense of freedom and lightness by gradually letting go of things that no longer served a purpose. Another minimalist, who chose to focus on experiences over possessions, shared how this shift in mentality brought clarity and peace. They cultivated a richer and more fulfilling life by valuing moments over material goods.

These examples highlight the potential for emotional decluttering to lead to profound personal transformation. By approaching the process with mindfulness and compassion, you can untangle the complex emotions that bind you to your possessions. In doing so, you open space—not just in your home but your life—for new experiences, relationships, and growth. It is important to avoid filling clear spaces with added items, as this does not address the underlying issue of clutter. Instead, focus on maintaining organization and preventing future accumulation. This path is not about erasing the past or denying its importance but about making room for what truly matters. The happiness of less becomes a concept and a lived reality, bringing a sense of calm and serenity.

1.4 The Science Behind ADHD and Organization

Understanding the science behind ADHD provides critical insight into the organizational challenges faced by those affected. ADHD is rooted in complex neurobiology, with executive function deficits playing a significant role. These deficits affect planning, prioritization, and task completion, making organization a persistent struggle. Research highlights the neurological basis of ADHD, pointing to differences in brain regions responsible for attention and impulse control. For example, the prefrontal cortex, which governs planning and decision-making, operates differently in individuals with ADHD. This knowledge underscores the unique hurdles in maintaining an organized space, where tasks often seem insurmountable due to the brain's wiring.

The intricate link between ADHD and clutter management becomes clearer.

When considering these scientific insights. The brain's difficulty in regulating tasks can lead to piles of unfinished business, while the struggle to maintain focus results in scattered efforts. Dopamine, a neurotransmitter linked to motivation and reward, is often dysregulated in ADHD. This dysregulation affects motivation and the ability to complete tasks, leading to procrastination and clutter. Recognizing these brain-based challenges allows for a more compassionate approach to clutter management. It shifts the narrative from personal failure to understanding the neurological underpinnings that influence the behavior.

Incorporating evidence-based strategies can significantly enhance organization for those with ADHD. Cognitive behavioral techniques are particularly effective in forming new habits and breaking unhelpful patterns. These techniques involve setting achievable goals, reinforcing positive behavior, and gradually building new routines. Visual aid also plays a crucial role in improving task management. Tools such as applying thought processes, for example, the choice of specific color-coded charts, lists, and calendars, can provide visual cues that help structure tasks and reduce cognitive load. By externalizing information, these aids make it easier to focus and complete tasks without being overwhelmed by the details.

Understanding the science of ADHD and its impact on the "organization|" of information empowers individuals to take effective action. This knowledge fosters increased self-awareness, allowing you to recognize patterns and triggers contributing to clutter. With this understanding comes self-compassion, acknowledging that the challenges faced are not a reflection of personal inadequacy but rather a byproduct of how the brain functions. With this insight, you can implement sustainable solutions tailored to your unique cognitive landscape. These strategies improve organizational skills and enhance overall well-being, fostering a sense of control and peace in daily life.

The benefits of understanding ADHD's scientific basis extend beyond just organization. They provide a foundation for holistic growth, where informed strategies lead to lasting change. As you embrace this knowledge, you gain the tools to create an environment that supports your strengths and accommodates your challenges. The path to an organized life is not about perfection but persistence and progress. Through science-backed strategies, you can build a clutter-free space that reflects clarity, purpose, and serenity. With each step, you move closer to a life where the chaos of clutter is replaced by a calm of order, empowering you to thrive in every aspect of your world.

Incorporating evidence-based strategies can significantly enhance organization for those with ADHD. Cognitive behavioral techniques (CBT) are particularly effective in forming new habits and breaking unhelpful patterns. By using what Rational vs Irrational is, CBT shows how negative thoughts can lead to negative feelings and actions. And if you think more positively and rationally, it can lead to more positive emotions and positive behaviors. Cognitive Behavioral Techniques involve setting achievable goals, reinforcing positive behavior, and gradually building new routines.

Visual aid also plays a crucial role in improving task management. Tools like color-coded charts, lists, and calendars can provide visual cues that help structure tasks and reduce cognitive load. By externalizing information, these aids make it easier to focus and complete tasks without being overwhelmed by the details.

Chapter 2: Preparing for the Decluttering Journey

"Out of clutter, find simplicity. From discord, find harmony. In the middle of difficulty lies opportunity."

— Albert Einstein

Imagine leaving, setting out on a grand voyage without a map or a known destination. It would feel daunting, overwhelming, and even impossible for some people. This is often how adults with ADHD feel when faced with decluttering. Here, I will start as I mean to go on, so I will equip you with a roadmap—setting realistic, achievable goals that transform this daunting task into a series of attainable steps. The trick to success lies in making goals, not just dreams, but concrete plans. This is where the S.M.A.R.T method shines—Specific, Measurable, Achievable, Relevant, and Time-bound goals. By clearly defining what success looks like, you give yourself a tangible target to aim for. Imagine saying, "I will organize the four shelves in my hall closet this Saturday morning." This specificity grounds your efforts, providing both direction and motivation. You will find that these small victories build momentum, each step helping you gain confidence and clarity in your decluttering process.

As you embark on this process, assessing your starting point accurately is vital. Think of it as taking an inventory, much like a shopkeeper would. Look around your living space and note the areas that most need attention. This might feel more like a scavenger hunt than a treasure hunt, but you identify clutter hotspots instead of collecting items. A clutter inventory helps highlight which areas are causing the most stress or hindrance in your daily life. Are your kitchen counters perpetually crowded? Is your closet overflowing with clothes? Identifying these high-priority areas allows you to focus on where they will make the most immediate impact, the wins you will appreciate the most!

Once you have mapped out your starting point, the next step is to break down the overwhelming task of decluttering into more manageable steps, chunking into doable bite-size 15-minute sessions! This is where creating a timeline becomes invaluable. Imagine dividing your tasks into small, bite-sized chunks, each taking no more than 15 minutes. This chunking method prevents you from feeling overwhelmed and helps you maintain focus. You might decide that Monday is for the kitchen drawers, Tuesday is for your desk, etc. Establishing a timeline creates a rhythm that keeps you engaged without overextending yourself.

Flexibility is equally essential in goal setting. Life is unpredictable, and sometimes your plans might need to change. An unexpected event disrupts your schedule, or you realize your goals are too ambitious. Revising your goals in response to progress—or lack thereof—is not a sign of failure but of adaptability. Celebrate your small wins, even if they seem minor. Every clear space is a victory, a step towards the calm and serenity you seek. Remember, it is not about perfection but progress.

Reflection Exercise: Crafting Your S.M.A.R.T Goals

Take a moment to sit down with a notebook or journal. Reflect on a specific area in your home that needs attention. Write down a S.M.A.R.T. goal for that space. Make sure it is Specific (What exactly will you accomplish?), Measurable (How will you know you've succeeded?), Achievable (Is it realistic given your resources?), Relevant (Does it matter to your overall decluttering mission?), and Time-bound (When will you complete it?). Revisit this goal regularly, adjusting as needed, and celebrate each step you take towards achieving it. This exercise is about organization and crafting a path to a more serene and fulfilling life.

2.2 Tools and Apps for a Clutter-Free Life

Technology can be your ally in the quest for a serene, clutter-free existence.

Digital tools, specifically designed to aid organization and time management, can transform how you approach decluttering. Take "Todoist," for example, an app that excels at task tracking. It helps you list your decluttering tasks, set priorities, and schedule reminders. This keeps you on track without feeling overwhelmed. For those who prefer visual organization, Trello offers an intuitive platform for project management. Imagine creating boards for each room or area in your home. You can add lists for tasks, categorize items, and move cards around as you progress. These apps streamline your efforts and inject a sense of accomplishment as tasks are completed and ticked off.

Lost Time is Never Found Again – Benjamin Franklin

While digital tools guide your organization, physical tools bring order into the tangible world. Consider the power of a label maker. It is a small investment that pays dividends in clarity and efficiency. Imagine opening your pantry to find neatly labeled jars and bins. Finding ingredients or supplies suddenly becomes a breeze, making your space more inviting. Storage bins also play a crucial role in sorting items. Opt for clear bins that allow you to see their contents briefly. This minimizes time spent searching and maximizes your ability to maintain order. By designating specific bins for distinct categories—such as donations, keepsakes, and recycling, you create a system that is easy to follow and sustain.

Integrating these tools into your daily routine can initially seem daunting, but it is about creating habits. You can start by setting reminders and alerts for decluttering sessions. Your smartphone or smartwatch can nudge you gently, ensuring that your 15-minute bursts do not get lost in the busyness of life. Use digital lists to track what needs to be done and what has been accomplished. This reduces paper clutter and makes it easier to update and reorganize your plans as needed. The key is consistency. Make these tools a natural part of your day, like checking emails or scrolling through social media.

Selecting the right tools involves considering your personal preferences and ADHD needs. First, how easy is it for you to use? An app or tool that seems overly complex is likely to be abandoned quickly. You can choose something intuitive that you can navigate with minimal effort. Accessibility is another factor. Ensure the tool is available across all your devices—phone, tablet, and computer. This allows you to synchronize and access your information wherever you are. Customization can also be crucial. Look for tools that let you tailor features to suit your workflow. Cross-device syncing is a bonus, ensuring that any changes you make on one device are reflected on all others, keeping your plans cohesive and up to date.

The right tools empower you to approach decluttering with newfound confidence and clarity. They provide structure and support, allowing you to focus on what matters most without being bogged down by chaos. As you explore these digital and physical aids, remember that the goal is to simplify your life, not complicate it. Choose what resonates with you, and let these tools guide you toward a clutter-free, peaceful environment where you can thrive.

2.3 Creating Your Personalized Decluttering Plan

Designing a decluttering plan that truly fits your lifestyle begins with understanding your strengths and weaknesses. This is not a one-size-fits-all approach. It is about tailoring a method that resonates with your daily rhythm and preferences. Please start by reflecting on past attempts to organize. What worked? What did not? You may find that tackling small areas boosts your morale, or you thrive on the satisfaction of completing a larger project. Recognizing these patterns helps craft a plan that plays to your strengths while addressing areas needing more support. Aligning this plan with your lifestyle ensures that decluttering becomes a sustainable habit, not just a dreaded chore.

Once you have assessed your approach, it is time to bring structure to your plans.

Please mark out your decluttering zones. You can do this by establishing specific decluttering zones throughout your home. Think of these zones as mini projects, each with its focus and purpose. This might mean dedicating a week to the kitchen, another to the bedroom, etc. Prioritize these areas based on their level of clutter and their relative impact on your daily life. A cluttered entryway, for example, can affect your mood every time you come home, making it a high-priority zone. This structured approach brings clarity to your process and ensures that you tackle the clutter in a logical, manageable, and prioritized way by tackling the zones that affect you most first.

In your planning, it is crucial to set boundaries and time limits. Without clear parameters, it is easy to become overwhelmed or burnt out. Decide how much time you will allocate to decluttering each day or week. This prevents the task from consuming your entire schedule and helps maintain balance. Setting a timer for 15-minute sessions can work wonders, allowing you to focus intensely without feeling drained.

Additionally, recognize when it might be time to seek help. Professional organizers can sometimes offer fresh perspectives and strategies you may not have considered. Alternatively, delegating tasks to a family member or friend can make the process more collaborative and less daunting.

Please review and adjust your plan regularly for continued progress. What works today might not be as effective next month, so be responsive to change. Conduct monthly Reviews to evaluate and assess what is working and what is not. This does not have to be lengthy; a simple checklist or a few notes in a journal can suffice. Use these reflections to make iterative improvements. Certain zones need revisiting, or a new tool could enhance efficiency. Flexibility in your approach allows for growth and adaptation, ensuring that your decluttering plan evolves with you.

Interactive Exercise: Zoning Your Space

Take some time to walk through your home with a notepad. Identify the zones that need attention and jot down what each area requires. Consider how these zones impact your daily life. Are there areas that cause you stress or disrupt your routine? Once identified, could you list them in order of priority? This exercise helps visualize your decluttering plan and provides a clear starting point. It is a practical step toward transforming your space into a haven of calm and organization. This is termed priority decluttering, whereby you have organized the decluttering based on its importance and impact on your life. Based on their ability to cause the most stress or disruption to your daily life.

2.4 Building a Supportive Environment

Creating an environment that nurtures and supports decluttering efforts can be transformative. The journey to a clutter-free life is not just about physical space but also about the emotional and psychological landscape that surrounds you. A supportive environment can significantly enhance your ability to declutter, offering encouragement and motivation to keep going even when challenges arise. Positive reinforcement from family and friends plays a critical role here. Imagine having a cheering squad ready to celebrate your victories, no matter how small. Their support can lift your spirits and encourage you to tackle even the most daunting tasks.

Designing a workspace that fosters focus is equally important. A clutter-free workspace signals to your brain that it is time for action. Minimizing distractions and creating a serene atmosphere paves the way for productivity and clarity. This could mean having a designated area for decluttering, free from the usual chaos, where you can concentrate without interruptions. A calm, organized space cultivates the mental clarity required to decide what to keep and let go of, making the process smoother and more enjoyable.

Family and friends can be more than just cheerleaders; they can actively participate in decluttering. Inviting them to join by organizing decluttering parties or challenges can transform a solitary task into a communal event. Collaborating on tasks makes the work feel easier and fosters a sense of camaraderie and shared purpose. Additionally, sharing your goals and progress with accountability partners can be highly effective. Knowing that you have someone to report back to creates a sense of responsibility, helping you stay on track while providing motivation and support.

Beyond personal connections, joining decluttering communities offers a wealth of benefits. In these circles, you will find others on the same path, facing similar challenges. Online forums and social media groups provide spaces to share stories, tips, and encouragement. Here, you can ask questions and receive advice from people who understand your struggles.

Local decluttering meetups or workshops offer opportunities to connect with others face-to-face, building a network of support that extends beyond the digital realm. These communities become a resource, a place to recharge and find inspiration when you need it most.

Maintaining a supportive environment is an ongoing process. Celebrate milestones together with loved ones to reinforce the progress you have made. Whether it is a small victory like clearing a desk or a more significant accomplishment like organizing a garage, acknowledging these achievements helps sustain motivation. Please seek new sources of inspiration and motivation, whether through books, podcasts, or conversations with your support network. Keeping the energy positive and encouraging ensures you stay engaged and dedicated to your decluttering goals.

As you build this supportive environment, remember that it is about creating a space where you feel empowered and motivated. Some people with ADHD discourage seeking support from their environment or using accountability partners from their local community, believing that it can lead to failure, much like a self-fulfilling prophecy. However, if something works for you, you should pursue it. The focus should be on taking small, positive steps moving forward. Rather than striving for perfection. Any positive results, no matter how small, should be recognized and rewarded.

This nurturing atmosphere will facilitate the decluttering process and enhance your overall well-being. With a dedicated support system, you are better equipped to face decluttering challenges and embrace the happiness of living in a serene, organized space.

With your environment ready to support your efforts, you will be in a better position to tackle the physical process of decluttering. In the next chapter, we will explore practical techniques for decluttering in short, manageable bursts, helping you maintain focus and motivation as you continue to live a clutter-free life.

Chapter 3: The 15-Minute Declutter Method
Finding Peace in Simplicity and Stories of Transformation

Imagine finding yourself in a room that feels like an endless sea of clutter, each item screaming for attention, yet none holding importance. This overwhelming scenario is familiar to many, especially those with ADHD. As you stand there, paralyzed by the chaos, diving into a major decluttering session can feel impossible. This is where the power of the 15-minute declutter method comes into play. Rather than overhauling an entire room or even a single closet in one go, this approach offers a manageable, bite-sized alternative. By focusing on short, concentrated bursts of activity, you can achieve "quick wins" that clear physical space and boost your mental state. Each 15-minute session is a small victory, a step towards regaining control and serenity in a chaotic world.

Setting a timer becomes an essential tool in this method, creating a sense of urgency and focus that can be remarkably effective. Knowing you have only 15 minutes helps reduce the indecision and procrastination that often accompany decluttering. You choose a specific, small area to tackle it, a single kitchen drawer or a section of your desk. These limited scopes prevent overwhelm and allow you to see immediate progress, which is crucial for maintaining motivation. Completing a task, no matter how small, a sense of accomplishment fuels further action.

There are many benefits to such short decluttering sessions. First, they boost motivation by offering tangible, visible results quickly. You might start with something as simple as organizing a drawer, but the impact on your mood and energy can be profound. There is a psychological relief in knowing that, in just a few minutes, you have created order where there was once chaos. Additionally, these short bursts significantly reduce decision fatigue. Limiting the scope of your task minimizes the mental strain of having to choose what to keep or discard. This leaves you feeling less drained and more inclined to continue decluttering.

To maximize efficiency in these short bursts, preparation is key. Gather any necessary tools beforehand — such as garbage bags for discards, bins for sorting, and cleaning supplies for tidying the area. Everything you need allows you to dive straight into the task without interruption. Focusing is also crucial. Set aside distractions and commit fully to the task at hand. Consider turning off notifications on your phone or setting it to "Do Not Disturb" mode to maintain concentration. Creating a focused environment ensures your 15 minutes are as productive as possible.

Real-life examples highlight the power of decluttering sprints. One reader shared how they transformed their kitchen by dedicating a series of 15-minute sessions to individual drawers and cabinets. Starting with the utensil drawer, they sorted through items, discarding duplicates and broken tools. The immediate sense of order was encouraging, and they moved on to tackle the spice rack in the next session. Another story comes from someone who organized a section of their closet by focusing on a single clothing category, such as t-shirts. They could make considerable progress without feeling overwhelmed by sorting, folding, and organizing within a confined time limit.

These examples are testaments to the effectiveness of the 15-minute declutter method. They show that even the most daunting clutter can be tackled with patience, persistence, and a strategic approach. As you embark on your decluttering journey, remember that each session is a step forward. Embrace the small victories that pave the way to a clutter-free, serene environment. With each 15-minute sprint, you clear physical space and carve out mental clarity and peace.

3.2 Task Chunking for ADHD Minds

When faced with a cluttered room, organizing it can want to climb a mountain. For those with ADHD, this sensation is often amplified, making it crucial to find strategies that simplify the process. Task chunking is a powerful tool in this respect. Decluttering becomes less daunting by breaking large tasks into smaller, manageable pieces. Imagine your living room as a series of zones rather than one overwhelming mess. By dividing it into areas—the coffee table, the couch, and the bookshelf—you create distinct targets to tackle one at a time. This segmentation transforms a hefty task into a series of smaller, achievable goals.

In addition to zoning, categorizing items can streamline decluttering by grouping items with similar fates. Suddenly, the room seems less chaotic, and your path becomes more explicit. This approach also alleviates the emotional weight of letting go by making decisions within a structured framework. It transforms the anxiety of parting with possessions into a more methodical and less emotionally charged process.

Task chunking offers significant cognitive benefits, especially for individuals with ADHD. By focusing on smaller tasks, you enhance your ability to maintain focus. The brain, which can quickly become overwhelmed by too many stimuli, finds concentrating on single, well-defined tasks easier. This singular focus reduces the cognitive load, making it easier to think clearly and act decisively. Moreover, task chunking simplifies the creation of a series of checkpoints that guide you through the process. This simplification helps mitigate feeling overwhelmed, allowing you to approach decluttering calmly and clearly.

Could you identify all tasks needed for a specific area to implement task chunking effectively? Please take a moment to survey your space and list tasks on a notepad or digital device. This might include clearing the coffee table, organizing books on the shelf, or puffing up the many cushions on the couch. Once you have your list, prioritize tasks based on urgency or importance. Decide which areas are most disruptive to your daily life and tackle those first. This prioritization ensures that your efforts have an immediate, positive impact, boosting your motivation to continue. By breaking tasks into these smaller, prioritized chunks, you create a roadmap that leads you step-by-step through the decluttering process.

Please look at how task chunking can be applied in various spaces. In a home office, for example, you might start with the desktop, clearing away papers and organizing supplies. From there, move to the drawers, sorting items into categories and discarding anything unnecessary. Finally, focus on filing important documents, ensuring they are easily accessible. In the bathroom, chunk tasks by organizing toiletries, towels, and cleaning supplies. This methodical approach allows you to transform each area from chaos to order without feeling overwhelmed by the entire space. Focusing on a tiny section at a time, you maintain motivation and clarity, steadily progressing toward a more organized home.

Task chunking is not just a strategy, but a mindset shift that empowers you to approach decluttering confidently and clearly. It transforms what once seemed like an insurmountable challenge into a series of manageable tasks, each bringing you closer to a clutter-free, serene environment. As you apply this technique, remember that each small success builds momentum, leading to lasting change.

3.3 Building Momentum with Daily Achievements

Imagine the satisfaction of ticking off a task from your to-do list. That small moment of triumph is more than just a fleeting feeling; it's a powerful motivator. Each daily achievement in decluttering contributes to lasting change, creating a ripple effect throughout your home and mind. For adults with ADHD, these achievements are particularly significant. They provide a sense of control and accomplishment, combating the chaos that clutter can bring. Completing even the most minor task can lift your spirits, injecting a dose of positivity into your day. It is not just about clearing space but about building a habit. This habit, cultivated through regular decluttering, transforms your environment into a haven of calm and order.

Setting daily decluttering goals is a strategic way to harness this power. You can start by selecting one small area or task to focus on daily. It might be as simple as tidying a drawer or organizing a bookshelf. The key is to choose something manageable, something you can accomplish without feeling overwhelmed. Creating a daily checklist can be immensely helpful. It provides structure and keeps you accountable. You see tangible proof of your progress as you tick off each completed task. This visual affirmation reinforces your efforts and keeps you motivated to continue.

Positive reinforcement plays a crucial role in sustaining this momentum. Celebrate your small wins, no matter how trivial they may seem. Each is a step forward, a building block in your journey towards a clutter-free life. You should consider rewarding yourself for completing daily goals. This does not have to be extravagant; a simple treat or a few moments of relaxation can suffice. Sharing your achievements with a supportive community can also amplify this effect. Whether it is friends, family, or an online group, having people cheer you on can boost your morale and drive you to persevere.

Picture this: you spend a few minutes each day organizing a section of your pantry. Over time, those brief efforts accumulate, transforming a chaotic mess into an artfully arranged space. Or you could dedicate your daily effort to tidying up your countertop, removing unnecessary items, and restoring orders. Each of these tasks, though small, contributes significantly to the overall harmony of your home. Daily victories build upon each other, leading to a profound sense of achievement.

The journey to decluttering does not have to be arduous. Focusing on daily achievements creates a rhythm of success that propels you forward. Each complete task boosts your confidence, proving that change is possible. This method makes the process much more manageable and infuses it with joy and satisfaction.

As you make these small yet positive strides, envision the clutter-free, serene environment that awaits. It is within your reach, one daily achievement at a time.

3.4 Overcoming Procrastination in Short Bursts

Procrastination can be a formidable foe, especially when confronted with clutter. For those with ADHD, it is often fueled by the fear of decision-making and a lack of immediate gratification. Imagine standing in front of a cluttered desk, overwhelmed by the sheer number of decisions. Each item you pick demands a choice—keep, toss, or donate. This fatigue can be paralyzing, leading to procrastination to avoid the discomfort of making choices. Additionally, it can be challenging to maintain motivation without the instant reward that comes from completing a task. The mountain of clutter remains, growing larger with each day of inaction.

To combat this, setting clear, short-term goals is crucial. Could you start by identifying just one specific task you can complete today? It might be as simple as sorting through a stack of papers or organizing a drawer. By narrowing your focus, you reduce the overwhelming nature of the task. The "5-minute rule" can be a powerful tool here. You can commit to working on a task for just five minutes. Often, the hardest part is starting; once you begin, you might find it easier to continue. This rule helps you break the inertia, making diving into more significant tasks less daunting. It is about tricking your brain into action, promising you can stop after five minutes if it pleases you, though you may find yourself motivated to keep going once you have started.

Author Margareta Magnussen coined the term 'Swedish death cleaning' in her 2018 book, *'The Gentle Art of Swedish Death Cleaning: How to Free Yourself and Your Family from a Lifetime of Clutter.'*

Swedish death cleaning, from the Swedish word *döstädning*, is a process of decluttering your household and preparing for the future with fewer things. Swedish culture believes in being prepared, and death cleaning is usually performed when someone's health declines or is close to retirement age.

"A loved one wishes to inherit nice things from you. Not all things from you." Hmm reminds me of that book titled D'ont Leave Your Shit or something along those lines!

Starting small is not only about easing into the process but also about building momentum. The compounding effect of small actions should not be underestimated. **Each tiny step forward creates a sense of progress, gradually leading to meaningful results.** Focusing on small tasks makes you chip away at the more substantial goal without feeling overwhelmed. This approach also reduces anxiety, as you are not facing the entire mountain of clutter at once. Instead, you're tackling it one pebble at a time, making the process more manageable and less intimidating.

Consider the story of a reader who overcame procrastination by applying these principles. Faced with a chaotic workspace, they set a five-minute timer each day. During this time, they focused solely on clearing their desks. Initially, it was just a few papers at a time, but gradually, their efforts expanded. Over weeks, those brief sessions transformed their workspace into an organized haven, free from the clutter that once stifled their productivity. Another individual tackled their cluttered living room by consistently dedicating short bursts of time to specific areas, such as the coffee table and bookshelves. The consistency of these efforts paid off, turning a once chaotic space into a calm, inviting environment. I have also used these methods with my brother to tackle his areas of clutter; it's helpful and a strong motivator to say hey, let us do this for 15 minutes, then we will stop! No matter what, you must stop after 15 minutes!

These narratives illustrate the power of small, intentional actions. They show that overcoming procrastination doesn't require monumental efforts. Instead, it's about finding strategies that work for you, starting small, and allowing those efforts to build over time. As you embrace these techniques, remember that each step, no matter how small, brings you closer to your goal of a clutter-free, serene environment. The Happiness of Less!

Chapter 4: Decluttering Key Living Spaces: Room by Room

Decluttering Mantra, How to Focus on What Truly Matters, Questions to Guide Every Decision, and The Process of Simplification

You can use your bedroom as a sanctuary, where you retreat to escape the day's demands. For many adults with ADHD, however, this space can become a source of stress rather than solace. A cluttered bedroom disrupts more than just the aesthetics of your space; it intrudes on your ability to relax and recharge. The bedroom should be a haven, fostering restful sleep and tranquility. Yet, for those with ADHD, the disorderly piles of clothes, stacks of unread books, and miscellaneous items can intensify anxiety, making it challenging to quiet the mind. By transforming your bedroom into a serene space, you reclaim control over your environment and, in turn, your mental well-being.

A clutter-free bedroom is paramount for achieving restful sleep, especially for individuals with ADHD. When your surroundings are chaotic, it can be challenging to unwind. Distractions in the form of clutter can keep your mind racing, preventing you from slipping into a peaceful slumber. By removing these distractions, you create an environment that promotes relaxation. This involves more than tidying up; it means making a space inviting calmness. Consider the impact of colors in your bedroom. Choose a calming color palette—soft blues, gentle greens, or warm neutrals—to soothe the senses and encourage tranquility. These colors create a backdrop that fosters serenity, helping to ease you into a restful state.

Wardrobe organization is crucial in simplifying daily routines and reducing the mental clutter often accompanying decision-making. Implementing seasonal wardrobe rotation can streamline this process. By storing out-of-season clothes out of sight, you minimize visual clutter and make it easier to choose outfits. This saves time and minimizes decision fatigue. Drawer dividers can further enhance organization, providing designated spaces for different clothing items. This simple addition ensures that each drawer serves a specific purpose, reducing the chaos that can ensue when searching for that one elusive sock or favorite sweater.

Nightstands, often the catch-all for miscellaneous items, can be transformed into functional spaces with a few strategic changes. Limit the items on your nightstand to essentials—a lamp, a book, a tiny plant. This minimalism reduces clutter and creates a sense of order. For additional storage, consider installing wall-mounted shelves. These provide space for items you may want nearby without cluttering surfaces. By keeping your bedside area clear, you foster a sense of calm that supports winding down at the end of the day.

A minimalist bedroom design emphasizes simplicity and functionality, creating a serene environment. Choose multi-functional furniture that maximizes space. A bed with built-in drawers or a bench with storage can reduce clutter while serving multiple purposes. Incorporating natural elements, such as plants, can also enhance the calming effect of your bedroom. Plants purify the air and bring a touch of nature indoors, creating a peaceful atmosphere. This simplicity in decor helps to clear both physical and mental clutter, providing a restful space that supports relaxation and rejuvenation.

Reflection Section: Designing Your Serenity Space

Could you take a moment to reflect on your bedroom? What elements contribute to tranquility, and what disrupts it? Consider the colors, the amount of clutter, and the functionality of the space. Write down your observations and identify minor changes you can make to enhance serenity. It's as simple as clearing your nightstand or introducing a calming color scheme. Use this reflection as a guide to transform your bedroom into a true sanctuary where you can unwind and recharge.

As you embark on this transformation, remember that the goal is not perfection but progress. Each minor change brings you closer to a bedroom that nurtures your well-being. The happiness of less is within reach, creating a space that genuinely supports relaxation.

4.2 Kitchen Clarity: Simplifying Meal Prep Areas

Imagine walking into your kitchen and immediately feeling a sense of calm. Everything has its place, and meal preparation flows effortlessly. A well-organized kitchen can be transformative, especially when life's demands pull you in multiple directions. For adults with ADHD, the kitchen can often become a chaotic zone, with misplaced items leading to stress and inefficiency. By categorizing pantry items, you create a navigable space that supports rather than hinders your cooking efforts. Group related items together, grains on one shelf, spices on another—and suddenly, finding what you need becomes a breeze. This simple organization minimizes the time spent searching, allowing you to focus on the joy of cooking rather than the chaos of clutter.

Designating specific zones for preparation, cooking, and cleaning can revolutionize how you navigate your kitchen. Each zone serves a distinct purpose, reducing the mental load of switching between tasks. Imagine a dedicated prep area with cutting boards and knives at the ready, a cooking zone with pots and pans within arm's reach, and a cleaning zone equipped with dishcloths and soap. This setup streamlines your workflow and reduces the likelihood of accidents, as you're not scrambling across the kitchen to grab what you need. These zones create a rhythm, turning what was once a stressful chore into an enjoyable activity.

Kitchen counters often become magnets for miscellaneous items, from mail to gadgets, creating visual chaos. Vertical storage solutions can be a game-changer for maintaining transparent surfaces. Wall-mounted racks or magnetic strips for utensils free up valuable counter space, keeping frequently used items accessible yet out of the way. Installing pull-out shelves inside cabinets can maximize storage efficiency. These shelves allow you to see and reach items at the back without unloading everything in front. This keeps your counters clear and reduces the time spent digging through cluttered cabinets.

Organizing your pantry and food storage requires attention to visibility and accessibility. Labeling containers with their contents and expiration dates transforms your pantry into a well-ordered library of ingredients. No more squinting at jars, wondering what lies inside. Implementing a first-in, first-out system for perishables ensures that older items are used before newer purchases, reducing waste and saving money. This system, standard in professional kitchens, can easily be adapted at home, providing a simple yet effective way to manage food inventory.

An efficient kitchen layout enhances functionality, making meal preparation seamless. Group related items, such as baking supplies or breakfast essentials, to create a logical flow. Placing frequently used items within easy reach reduces unnecessary movement and keeps your focus on cooking rather than searching. Imagine opening a cabinet and immediately spotting the pot you need or reaching for spices without shuffling through a drawer of mismatched jars. This accessibility saves time and makes cooking more enjoyable, as everything you need is right where you expect it to be.

4.3 Creating a Zen Zone in Your Living Room

Now imagine a corner of your living room dedicated solely to relaxation, a sanctuary amid the daily hustle. This concept, often called a Zen Zone, is about carving out a space where stress melts away and tranquility reigns. In selecting your Zen Zone, you should consider seating that invites comfort. A plush armchair or a cozy love seat adorned with soft throws can become your retreat. The seating should cradle you, providing a place to unwind with a book or reflect on the day. Soft lighting further enhances this ambiance, casting a gentle glow that soothes the senses. A floor lamp with an adjustable dimmer or a string of fairy lights can transform the atmosphere, creating a cocoon of calmness.

Decluttering your living area is key to maintaining a minimalist and functional environment. You can begin by evaluating decorative items. Often, surfaces are cluttered with trinkets and knick-knacks that add little value to space. Instead, could you reduce these to a few meaningful pieces that resonate with you? A photograph that invokes cherished memories or a sculpture that inspires tranquility. This selective approach clears visual clutter and imbues the space with personal significance. Like storage ottomans, multifunctional furniture can also contribute to a minimalist design. These pieces serve dual purposes, offering seating or footrests while concealing items inside. This dual functionality keeps your space tidy without sacrificing style or comfort.

Organizing media and entertainment centers require careful planning. The large number of cables can become tangled and unsightly, affecting the room's appearance. Invest in cable management solutions to keep them neatly tucked away, maintaining a clean look. Velcro ties or cable sleeves can work wonders here, streamlining the appearance of your setup. For books and media, consider arranging them by category or theme. This makes finding what you need more manageable and adds a sense of order and sophistication. Grouping books by color or size can be visually pleasing, turning your media center into a focal point rather than a cluttered mess.

A balanced living room layout enhances both functionality and harmony. Thoughtful furniture arrangement creates a space where movement flows effortlessly. Please ensure that all pathways throughout the home remain clear, allowing for natural and unobstructed navigation throughout. This approach prevents an area from feeling cramped, allowing you to move freely and comfortably. Could you create distinct areas for different activities? A reading nook with a lamp and a small table, a spot for watching TV with comfortable seating, or a corner for creative pursuits. Each area serves a purpose, contributing to an overall sense of balance and serenity.

By incorporating these elements into your living room, you establish a Zen Zone that transforms your space into a haven of relaxation. This isn't about appearance but cultivating an environment that supports mental clarity and peace. The living room, often the heart of the home, becomes a place where you can unwind, recharge, and find solace amid the chaos of everyday life.

4.4 Streamlining Your Home Office for Focus

Your home office is more than just a workplace; it's a command center for productivity. For adults with ADHD, a clutter-free workspace is key to maintaining focus and efficiency. Imagine sitting down at work and finding everything in its place. The absence of clutter allows your mind to settle, reducing distractions and enabling you to concentrate on the tasks. Setting up a designated work zone is crucial. This means setting aside a specific area solely for work, free from the distractions of daily life. Whether it's a corner of your living room or a separate room, having a dedicated space signals your brain that it is time to focus. Personalize this space to boost motivation. Add inspiring elements, like a favorite painting or a small plant. This personalization can increase your sense of ownership and make the space more inviting.

A tidy desk area is vital for maintaining a functional workspace. You can use drawer organizers for pens, stationery, and other office supplies. These organizers keep items arranged, making it easy to find what you need without sifting through cluttered drawers. A well-organized desk fosters a sense of control, reducing stress and allowing you to dive into work quickly. Implementing a filing system for important documents is equally important. Categorize papers into folders or binders, ensuring each has a clear label. This system keeps your desk clear and saves time when locating specific documents. Regularly review your files, discarding what's unnecessary to prevent accumulation.

Digital clutter can be just as disruptive as physical clutter. To manage this, regularly declutter your computer desktop and folders. A cluttered screen can overwhelm your senses, making it difficult to focus on your work. You can take time each week to organize files, delete those you no longer need, and arrange the rest into clearly labeled folders. This practice keeps your digital workspace neat and functional. You should consider using cloud storage for easy access to files. Services like Google Drive or Dropbox allow you to store documents online, freeing up space on your device and making accessing your work from anywhere easier. This setup also serves as a backup, ensuring your important files are safe and accessible even if your computer encounters issues.

Ergonomic office design plays a pivotal role in promoting comfort and productivity. You can choose an adjustable chair and desk that support proper posture. A chair with lumbar support and a desk at the correct height can prevent strain and fatigue, allowing you to work comfortably for extended periods. Incorporating natural light into your workspace can also have a significant impact. You can position your desk near a window, as natural light reduces eye strain and boosts mood. If natural light is limited, use adjustable lamps that mimic daylight to illuminate your workspace effectively. This setup creates a pleasant environment conducive to sustained focus and productivity.

In conclusion, a well-organized home office tailored to your needs can transform how you work. Creating a designated work zone and maintaining physical and digital order lays the groundwork for improved focus and efficiency. An ergonomic setup enhances comfort, while personal touches make the space inviting. As you streamline your home office, you're not just clearing clutter but setting the stage for success, enabling you to tackle tasks with clarity and confidence. With these strategies, your home office becomes a sanctuary of productivity, supporting your goals and enhancing your daily life.

Chapter 5: Tackling Emotional and Sentimental Clutter

Imagine opening a box filled with old letters, photographs, and keepsakes. Each item holds a story, a connection to a moment in time that feels irreplaceable. For many, these objects are more than just things; they are tangible pieces of our lives. For adults with ADHD, the emotional ties to such items can be even more profound, often leading to a cluttered space that is difficult to part with. However, the journey to a clutter-free life involves not just physical decluttering but also addressing the sentimental attachments that bind us to our belongings. It's here that mindful reflection can become a powerful tool, helping individuals acknowledge their emotional connections while making thoughtful decisions about what to keep and what to let go.

Mindful reflection encourages you to pause and consider each item's role. By taking a moment to reflect, you can appreciate the memories and experiences that these objects represent. Practicing gratitude during decluttering sessions allows you to honor the past without feeling burdened. This process can ease the emotional burden of parting with belongings as you focus on the joy and lessons these items have brought rather than the loss of letting them go. Gratitude helps reduce guilt or regret as you acknowledge the item's contribution to your journey and readiness to move on. This approach cultivates a sense of peace and closure, allowing you to release the item with kindness and appreciation.

Incorporating mindfulness into your decluttering process can be both simple and transformative. Begin with a breathing exercise to center your focus before starting. Take a few deep breaths, inhaling calm and exhaling stress, to ground yourself in the present moment. This practice clears your mind, allowing you to approach the task clearly and intentionally. Consider writing a gratitude journal entry for each as you encounter sentimental items. Reflect on the memories associated with the item, the experiences it represents, and the emotions it evokes. This exercise transforms decluttering from a chore into a meaningful ritual that honors the past while embracing the future.

The power of mindful decluttering is evident in the stories of those who have embraced this approach. One individual shared their experience of letting go of childhood memorabilia. As they sorted through boxes of old toys and school projects, they paused to reflect on each item's significance. By writing down memories and expressing gratitude, they found the courage to part with many of these objects, keeping only those that truly resonated. This process cleared physical space and freed mental energy, allowing them to focus on creating new memories in the present.

Another story comes from someone who found joy in simplicity through mindful decluttering. For years, they held on to items for fear of forgetting essential moments. However, as they practiced gratitude and reflection, they discovered that memories reside not in objects but in the heart and mind. They could release possessions by focusing on the emotions and experiences that mattered most, finding a sense of liberation and peace. This shift in perspective brought clarity and joy, transforming their relationship with their belongings and environment.

These narratives highlight the profound impact that mindfulness and gratitude can have on the decluttering process. By approaching your belongings with thoughtfulness and appreciation, you open yourself to the possibility of living with "less" yet feeling enriched by the memories and experiences that truly matter. As you embark on your journey of mindful decluttering, remember that each item you release makes room for new opportunities and growth, paving the way for a more serene and fulfilling life.

Reflection Exercise: Gratitude Journaling for Sentimental Items

Please set aside a few minutes to reflect on a sentimental item you wish to declutter. Please write down the memories it evokes, the emotions it stirs, and the lessons it has imparted. Express gratitude for its role in your life, acknowledging the joy and growth it has contributed. Consider how letting go of this item might open space for new experiences and memories. This exercise is about releasing objects and embracing the happiness of less, nurturing a life filled with intention and meaning.

5.2 Emotional Clutter: Identifying and Addressing Attachments

Emotional clutter is a unique challenge in decluttering, distinct from the physical mess surrounding us. While physical clutter consists of the tangible items that crowd our spaces, emotional clutter is rooted in the psychological bonds we form with our possessions. These items are kept not out of need or desire but due to obligation, nostalgia, or guilt. You feel obligated to keep the old gift from a long-lost friend or the artifact passed down. Such belongings often trigger negative emotions or memories, making it difficult to decide their fate. They occupy not just physical space but also mental real estate, contributing to stress and reducing clarity.

Recognizing these emotional attachments is the first step in addressing them. Start by reflecting on the source of each attachment. Ask yourself whether the item is tied to a specific memory, a sense of duty, or nostalgia. Understanding the root of the connection can provide insight into whether the item truly serves your current life or is merely a relic of the past holding you back. Consider asking critical questions: Why do I keep this? How does it serve me today? These questions help you evaluate the value of your possessions, distinguishing between those that enrich your life and those that weigh you down. They foster a sense of awareness, allowing you to see your belongings through a lens of purpose rather than sentimentality.

Once you have identified the emotional ties, developing strategies to address emotional clutter becomes essential. Begin by setting boundaries for sentimental items. Determine a specific space or area where these items will reside, preventing them from encroaching on other parts of your home. This might mean designating a single shelf for keepsakes or limiting the number of mementos you allow yourself to keep. Establishing these limits creates a sense of order and control, reducing the chaos that emotional clutter can bring. Another effective strategy is reframing your perspective on the necessity of keeping certain items. Instead of viewing them as indispensable, consider how letting go might liberate you from the past, making room for new experiences and growth. This shift in mindset can transform the daunting task of decluttering into an opportunity for personal development and renewal.

Addressing emotional clutter offers numerous benefits for your overall well-being. You'll notice increased mental clarity and stress reduction as you release items that no longer serve you. The weight of obligation and guilt that once accompanied these items dissipates, leaving you with a sense of freedom and lightness. This clarity enhances your ability to focus on present and future goals, unburdened by the remnants of the past. It allows you to channel your energy into pursuits that align with your true intentions and aspirations, fostering a sense of purpose and fulfillment.

Imagine the relief of entering a space that no longer holds the echoes of unfinished business or unresolved emotions. This liberation is not just about having a tidy room; it's about achieving a state of mind where peace and clarity reign. As you navigate the complexities of emotional clutter, remember that the process is not about erasing memories but honoring them and allowing yourself to move forward unencumbered. Releasing emotional attachments is a powerful act of self-care, empowering you to create an environment that truly reflects who you are today and who you aspire to become.

5.3 The Happiness of Less: Finding Joy in Simplicity

Imagine waking up in a home where every item you own serves a clear purpose, space breathes with openness, and the burden of excess no longer weighs you down. This is the heart of finding happiness in simplicity, a philosophy that can transform how you live and experience the world around you. The minimalist mindset encourages prioritizing experiences over possessions, valuing the moments that shape us rather than the objects that merely fill space. By embracing a lifestyle that favors quality over quantity, you begin to see the richness life offers when you let go of the unnecessary. This shift is not about deprivation but about making room for what enriches your life.

The psychological benefits of living with less are profound and well-documented. Research suggests that simplicity can significantly reduce anxiety and increase contentment. When you rid yourself of excess, you also eliminate the visual noise and chaos contributing to stress. A study on minimalism linked it to lower cortisol levels, the hormone associated with stress, highlighting how a clutter-free environment nurtures a more peaceful state of mind. Real-life examples abound of individuals who thrive with less and find that reducing their possessions leads to enhanced clarity and focus. They report feeling a sense of liberation and joy, freed from the constant pressure to accumulate more. These individuals often find that with fewer distractions, they can engage more deeply in relationships and personal growth, fostering a richer and more fulfilling life.

To cultivate a minimalist mindset, start by setting intentional living goals that align with your values and passions. Reflect on what truly matters to you and let this guide your decisions about what to keep and release. Practicing mindful consumption is another vital step. Before acquiring the latest items, consider their purpose and impact on your life. Ask yourself if they contribute to your goals or if they might become just another piece of clutter. This mindful approach helps build a life filled with intention and purpose, where every possession serves a meaningful role.

The stories of transformation through decluttering and minimalism are both inspiring and instructive. Consider the individual who moved from a life of clutter and chaos to one of clarity and balance. By systematically reducing their belongings, they discovered a newfound sense of freedom. They no longer felt tethered to their possessions, allowing them to focus on personal growth and meaningful relationships. This journey to simplicity was not about loss but about gaining physical and mental space for what truly matters. The impact of this simpler lifestyle extended beyond the home, influencing their personal and professional lives. With less to manage and maintain, they found more time and energy to pursue passions, connect with loved ones, and engage deeply in their community.

Another narrative involves someone who embraced minimalism after realizing the toll that clutter had taken on their well-being. They found that by letting go of superfluous items, they could better appreciate the beauty and utility of what remained. This shift brought profound joy and purpose as their living space reflected their values and aspirations. Their relationships flourished as they prioritized experiences over material possessions, fostering connections grounded in presence and authenticity.

These transformations underscore the joy and fulfillment that come from simplicity. By embracing the happiness of less, you open yourself to a life rich with joy, purpose, and connection. This isn't about decluttering your home; it's about decluttering your life and making room for the experiences, relationships, and growth that truly matter. As you explore this path, remember that simplicity is not an endpoint but a way of living that continuously enriches your life and the lives of those around you.

5.4 Techniques for Handling Sentimental Keepsakes

Letting go of sentimental items can feel like losing a piece of your history. Each object tells a story, holding memories of moments and people that have shaped your life. For adults with ADHD, these keepsakes often evoke powerful emotions, and deciding to part with them is a complex one. Losing those memories can be daunting as if discarding an item somehow erases the experiences it represents. Balancing sentimental value with practicality becomes a struggle, leading to a home filled with cherished yet overwhelming clutter. This emotional weight can be a significant barrier to achieving the serenity of a clutter-free space.

Practical techniques can offer guidance to navigate this challenge. You can start by creating a memory box for your most cherished items. This box becomes a sanctuary for objects with profound meaning, allowing you to preserve those special memories without letting them dominate your living space. Limit the box size to keep only the most significant items. Another effective strategy is digitizing photos and documents. By scanning pictures and important papers, you retain the memories while freeing up physical space. This approach makes it easier to revisit those memories whenever you wish, without the burden of physical storage.

Finding a balance between holding on to sentimental items and maintaining an organized home. Compromise is key. You can allow yourself limited space for sentimental collections, dedicating a specific shelf or corner to display them. This boundary keeps these items from spreading throughout your home, maintaining order while honoring your emotional connections. You should consider rotating sentimental displays to keep memories fresh and meaningful. By changing which items are displayed every few months, you can enjoy different memories at various times, preventing them from becoming part of the unnoticed background. This practice revitalizes your space and allows you to appreciate each item more deeply when it's in focus.

Consider the story of a family who successfully organized their heirlooms. Faced with generations of keepsakes, they decided to focus on what truly mattered. They selected a few key pieces to display prominently, while others were carefully packed into labeled boxes for safe storage. This selective approach allowed them to honor their heritage without feeling overwhelmed. Another example is of individuals who have embraced digital memory keeping. By scanning old letters and photographs, they preserved the essence of their past while clearing physical space. This reduced clutter and provided peace of mind, knowing their memories were securely stored and easily accessible.

These stories illustrate that handling sentimental keepsakes does not mean losing your past. Instead, it's about curating the memories that truly resonate, creating a home that reflects who you are today. By balancing holding on and letting go, you create a space that honors your history while supporting your present and future. Balancing involves managing emotions and cherishing meaningful parts of your life without excess. Keeping items, you're not ready to let go of is fine. The goal is not to purge but to create a living space that nurtures your well-being and growth.

In managing sentimental keepsakes, you learn to appreciate your past without letting it define your present. This approach fosters a sense of peace, transforming your home into a sanctuary of cherished memories and new possibilities. As you continue to declutter, you make room for the happiness of less, embracing a life where every item has purpose and meaning. The journey through sentimental clutter is a step toward a more serene and fulfilling existence where simplicity can bring profound joy and peace. An existence where your surroundings reflect the life you wish to lead. With this clarity, you are better prepared to face the remaining spaces.

Chapter 6: Maintaining Motivation and Focus

For this next exercise, please imagine you are taking a stand in the middle of a room in your home, and you see it is cluttered and chaotic, a space that demands more time and energy than you can muster. Yet, amidst this disorder lies an untapped superpower— yes, it is the ability to hyperfocus. For individuals with ADHD, hyperfocus is a state where intense concentration on a task can lead to remarkable productivity and precision. It is as if the entire world can be blocked out whilst you are obsessed with a new interest in your life. Yes, that is hyperfocus; this becomes a powerful ally in decluttering, turning what feels like an insurmountable challenge into an opportunity for deep cleaning and organization, often with an efficiency that surprises even the most seasoned declutter aficionado.

Hyperfocus allows you to hone in on specific tasks and complete them with a level of detail and thoroughness that other methods struggle to achieve. When the hyperfocus kicks in, distractions seem to disappear by the wayside, and you focus your mind on the task at hand, producing a seamless flow of productivity. This state of hyperfocus harnesses your attention and directs it toward one goal. **The precision and efficiency that come with hyperfocus can instantly transform a cluttered room into a well-organized space in a fraction of the time it usually takes**. By utilizing this intense focus to concentrate, greater satisfaction and accomplishment are experienced as it works its magic.

It is a marvelous ability to tap into hyperfocus; first, identify the area you wish to work on, which naturally captivates your interest. It could be organizing your book collection by genre or color or sorting through your wardrobe to create a capsule collection once you've pinpointed the hyperfocus by minimizing distractions, turning off notifications, or putting them too silent. Setting a specific goal for your session can also help, providing a clear target to aim for and a sense of direction.

One key benefit of using hyperfocus in decluttering is its ability to facilitate deep cleaning in a single session. When hyperfocus takes over, you can tackle a project you have avoided for months, such as organizing a garage. The intense concentration allows you to work systematically, item by item, transforming an overwhelming area into a space of order and calm. The immediate, tangible results can be incredibly motivating, reinforcing the desire to continue decluttering.

Consider the story of a reader who channeled hyperfocus to declutter their garage daily. What had once been a chaotic storage space filled with forgotten tools and seasonal decorations became a well-organized area where everything had its place. The reader described a profound sense of accomplishment and relief from the physical transformation and the mental clarity it brought. Another example involves someone who applied hyperfocus to their home office. They created a workspace that enhanced productivity and reduced stress by dedicating a focused session to reorganizing files, supplies, and digital clutter.

While hyperfocus is not a state you can summon at will, you can harness this powerful tool to make significant strides in decluttering endeavors by understanding and creating conditions that support it. As you explore the potential of hyperfocus, remember that the goal is not to achieve perfection but to make progress, one focused session at a time.

6.2 Motivation Maintenance: Keeping the Fire Alive

Maintaining motivation amid decluttering can often feel like a steep uphill climb. The initial rush of excitement when starting the process is invigorating, but the spark that worked for you can quickly fade as soon as time passes. This waning enthusiasm is a common hurdle, especially when early progress seems slow, or the sheer amount of clutter feels insurmountable. External distractions and competing priorities can further drain motivation, making it challenging to stay focused. A work commitment suddenly demands your attention, or a family matter requires your energy, pushing decluttering to the back burner. In these moments, it is crucial to recognize that motivation is not a constant force but requires nurturing and renewal.

To keep motivation alive, you must set regular reminders for yourself. These could be simple alarms on your phone or notes on your calendar, prompting you to engage in a small decluttering task each day. Pairing these reminders with rewards for completing tasks, no matter how small, can also be effective. The reward does not have to be elaborate; it could be as simple as allowing yourself a few minutes of relaxation or enjoying a favorite treat. These strategies can help you stay on track and maintain enthusiasm over time.

Tracking your progress visually with charts or apps can also be incredibly motivating. Seeing a visual representation of your accomplishments can provide a sense of achievement and encourage you to keep going. Consider using a decluttering app that allows you to list goals and check them off as you complete them or create a physical chart where you can mark your progress with colorful stickers or pens. These tangible signs of progress serve as positive reinforcement, helping to maintain enthusiasm over time.

"The best way to find out what we need is to get rid of what we don't."

— Marie Kondo

Accountability partners can play a pivotal role in sustaining motivation. Sharing your decluttering goals and updates with friends or family provides a sense of responsibility and encouragement. When others know your goals, they can support, celebrate your successes, and gently nudge you when needed. Some People with ADHD, however, claim it is not recommended you have accountability partners as it is one sure way to set yourself up for inevitable failures. The self-fulfilling prophecy can come into play. Joining decluttering groups online or in your community can also provide mutual encouragement. In these groups, you will find others who understand your challenges and can offer advice, share experiences, and cheer you on. The camaraderie and shared commitment to decluttering can be incredibly uplifting, making the process feel less solitary and more like a collective endeavor.

Motivational success stories can serve as powerful reminders of what is possible. Take the example of a family who decided to tackle their clutter together. By setting aside time each weekend to focus on a different area of their home, they made noteworthy progress and strengthened their family bonds. Each family member had a role, and they celebrated the small victories of the family. Their home became more organized and serene, bringing them closer. Another inspiring story is about an individual who aims to complete a room-by-room challenge. They gradually transformed their entire home by dedicating 15 minutes daily to a specific task in different rooms. The sense of accomplishment from each completed room fueled their motivation to continue, leading to a clutter-free, harmonious living environment.

These examples highlight the impact of consistent effort and the power of a supportive network. They show that motivation can be sustained through deliberate actions and community support, turning what once felt like an overwhelming task into a rewarding and transformative experience.

6.3 Overcoming Decision Fatigue with Simple Strategies

"Out of clutter, find simplicity. From discord, find harmony. In the middle of difficulty lies opportunity."

— Albert Einstein

Just imagine yourself standing in a room filled with clutter, and each item demands a decision. Do you keep, donate, recycle, or toss it? This is where decision fatigue rears its ugly head, a phenomenon that can significantly hinder your progress in decluttering. Decision fatigue occurs when the mental energy required for making numerous choices leads to exhaustion. This fatigue can become a threatening barrier, especially for individuals with ADHD, as it makes even the most straightforward decisions feel overwhelming. Frustration mounts when faced with too many choices, and procrastination becomes an easy escape. **The more decisions you face, the harder it becomes to choose, leading to a cycle of delayed action and increased clutter.**

To counteract decision fatigue, introducing structured decision-making frameworks can be incredibly helpful. These frameworks reduce the cognitive load **by simplifying the decision process. One such approach is the "one-touch rule,"** which encourages you to handle each item only once before deciding. This method eliminates the tendency to move items from one pile to another without resolution. By committing to a decision the first time you touch an item, you reduce the number of decisions made and **streamline the decluttering process**. Another effective strategy is the "two-minute rule." If a decision or action can be completed in two minutes or less, please do it as soon as possible. This rule helps tackle small tasks that might otherwise accumulate, contributing to clutter and decision fatigue. Then there is the 20/80 Pareto rule, whereby only 20 % of the stuff we own is used. The rest is surplus to requirements, quite literally!

Several rules could be used to simplify your choices further, thereby alleviating the burden of decision fatigue. You can begin by categorizing items before you sort. By grouping related items, you create a clearer picture of what you own, making it easier to identify duplicates or unnecessary possessions. This categorization streamlines the process and reduces the number of individual decisions you must make. Establishing clear criteria for keeping or discarding items also aids decision-making. Consider questions such as: Does this item serve a purpose? Does it bring joy or hold significant sentimental value? Setting these criteria beforehand minimizes the mental effort required during decluttering, leading to more efficient and confident decisions.

Reducing decision fatigue offers numerous benefits in your decluttering efforts. With fewer choices, progress is faster and involves less mental strain. This efficiency means you can accomplish more in your 15-minute sessions, seeing tangible results more quickly. The simplification of decisions can boost one's confidence in the choices made, as you are no longer second-guessing every move. This newfound confidence can be empowering, transforming decluttering from a daunting task into a manageable and enjoyable activity. With decision fatigue minimized you can approach your space with clarity and purpose, making informed decisions that align with your goals for a calm and organized home.

Imagine the relief of entering a room where each item has a place, where your decisions have shaped a space that reflects your intentions and values. As decision fatigue diminishes, your ability to create a serene and clutter-free environment grows, leading to greater calmness and satisfaction in your daily life. With simple strategies and structured choices, you can conquer the chaos and embrace the Happiness of less.

6.4 Visualizing Success: The Power of a Clutter-Free Mindset

Visualize and use your imagination to facilitate a decluttered home where every item has its place, transparent surfaces, and the air feels light. **Imagination is a powerful tool that can help make dreams become reality as you create a mental blueprint that guides your actions.** Visualization is more than daydreaming; it is a focused exercise that enhances motivation and concentration. When you mentally walk through your ideal living space, noticing the tidy shelves, the uncluttered floors, and the serene atmosphere, you set a clear intention for what you want to achieve. Creating a vision board can be an effective way to represent these decluttering goals. You can use images and words that embody tranquility and imagine what you see in your home. This board constantly reminds you of your aspirations, keeping you focused and inspired as you work towards a clutter-free environment.

You can set aside dedicated time for these sessions to practice visualization effectively. Find a quiet, comfortable spot where you will not be disturbed. Close your eyes and take a few deep breaths to center yourself. As you visualize your space, incorporate sensory details to make the experience vivid. Imagine the soothing colors of your walls, the soft texture of your couch, or the fresh scent of a well-organized kitchen. Engage all your senses to create a rich, immersive, almost tangible image. This vividness helps solidify your goals, making them feel more achievable. Regular practice of these visualization exercises can strengthen your commitment to decluttering, turning abstract desires into actionable plans.

The psychological benefits of visualization extend beyond motivation. Maintaining a clear picture of your desired outcome increases your determination. This clarity provides a guiding light, helping you navigate obstacles with confidence and resolve. When challenges arise, as they inevitably will, the vision of your ideal home serves as a guiding touchstone, a force to remind you of why you started and what you stand to gain. This visualization focus can be particularly empowering for individuals with ADHD, as it channels your energy and attention towards a single, meaningful goal.

Consider the story of a reader who regularly visualizes their ideal living space. Each morning, they spent a few minutes imagining their home as they wished it to be, filled with light and order. This mental exercise focused on their goals, influencing their daily actions and choices. Over time, their living space began to reflect this manifestation, each minor change accumulating into a significant transformation. Similarly, another individual focused on visualizing a serene cooking area in their chaotic kitchen. Holding on to this image inspired them to tackle one section at a time, gradually turning their cluttered kitchen into a calm, efficient space. These examples illustrate how visualization can transform not just your environment but also your approach to decluttering.

As you embrace visualization, remember that it is a tool to help guide your efforts, not a substitute for action. You can use these mental images to inspire and motivate you, providing directions as you work towards a clutter-free home. If you keep your vision clear and your goals in sight, you empower yourself to create a living space that reflects your values and aspirations. Just note that every step you take brings you closer to the Happiness and serenity of having less.

Use your visualization skills to tackle decluttering challenges. As you progress, harness clarity and motivation, letting them guide you toward a more organized and fulfilling life.

With visualization as a powerful ally, you are well-equipped to tackle decluttering challenges. As you progress, harness this clarity and motivation, letting it guide you toward a more organized and fulfilling life.

Chapter 7: Digital Decluttering for Mental Clarity

If you picture this, your phone buzzes, a notification lights up, and suddenly, you are pulled away from the task at hand, and your focus is lost instantly.

This cycle repeats, leaving you feeling scattered, all over the place, and overwhelmed. For adults with ADHD, the digital world can be particularly distracting, contributing to stress and reducing focus. However, it is very possible to regain control and clarity by embarking on a digital detox. This concept involves intentionally disconnecting from devices to refresh your mind and reduce stress.

Why is this necessary? In today's hyper-connected era, digital detoxes provide much-needed relief from the constant influx of information. They allow you to reset, helping you refocus on what truly matters. Just as clutter in your home can cause chaos, digital clutter can overwhelm your mental space, making it difficult to concentrate and function effectively.

Unplugging from the digital world helps you reclaim your mental health, allowing you to breathe and rediscover the joys of being present.

The benefits of unplugging are profound. When you step away from screens, you reduce exposure to the constant stimuli that can overtax your brain. This break allows your mind to rest, decreasing stress levels and improving overall mood. Without the distraction of notifications, you can engage more fully with the world around you, enhancing your relationships and boosting your productivity. Unplugging also helps reset your brain's dopamine levels, which can become overstimulated by endless digital interactions. This reset improves focus and concentration, paving the way for more meaningful and intentional engagement with technology when you return.

Setting boundaries for digital consumption, just as you would with children, is crucial in returning to what is real. You should, without a doubt, establish tech-free zones or times in your home when devices are banned. The dining room may become a no-phone zone; encouraging mealtime conversations after all sitting down together at mealtimes and communicating with each other is or should be something we all strive for. Or you can designate an hour before bed as screen-free, allowing your mind to wind down and prepare for restful sleep. These boundaries create a healthier relationship with technology, reminding you that not every moment needs to be filled with digital noise.

Instead, look for opportunities for offline activities, such as reading a book, walking, or enjoying a hobby or sport. These moments of disconnection foster creativity and mindfulness, enriching your life in ways that screens cannot.

The methods utilized to detox should involve a structured plan for when you plan to reduce technological interactions temporarily. Please let friends and family know about your intentions so they understand your absence from the digital world. That way, they do not panic when you don't respond as usual. This communication sets expectations and reduces pressure to respond immediately to messages or emails.

Find alternative activities to fill the time traditionally spent online. It could be a new fitness routine, exploring nature, or spending quality time with loved ones. Engaging in these offline pursuits helps you reconnect with yourself and those around you, strengthening personal bonds and enhancing well-being.

The impact of digital clutter on mental health is significant. Constant emails and social media notifications create a perpetual state of alertness, making it difficult to relax and focus. This digital noise contributes to overwhelm and distractibility, particularly for individuals with ADHD. The pressure of being constantly "on" and available can lead to burnout, as your brain struggles to process the endless stream of information. Reducing digital interactions alleviates this electronic device stress, giving your mind the space to function optimally.

I do not know about anyone who has not gained from a digital detox. Success stories abound of individuals who have benefited from digital detox practices. Consider how one family that adopted weekly tech-free evenings discovered the joy of board games, storytelling, and deep conversations, strengthening their connections without the interference of screens.

Another narrative involves a weekend retreat spent entirely offline. Participants reported feeling rejuvenated and more focused, with a renewed appreciation for the world around them. These experiences highlight the transformative power of stepping away from technology, if only temporarily.

Reflection Section: Planning Your Digital Detox,

Please look at your current relationship with technology. Are there areas where digital interactions feel overwhelming or intrusive? Set aside time to plan a digital detox. Identify tech-free zones or times and choose offline activities that bring you joy. Record your intentions in a journal, noting any anticipated challenges and how you plan to overcome them. Reflect on the potential benefits of this disconnection, envisioning the clarity and calm it might bring. Use this reflection to guide your digital detox, welcoming the peace and presence of stepping away from screens.

As you explore the idea of a digital detox, remember that it's not about eliminating technology. Instead, it's about creating a balanced relationship that enhances your life rather than detracting you from it. Embrace the opportunity to reset and recharge, finding serenity in the space between the Beep, beep buzzing notifications!

7.2 Organizing Your Virtual Workspace

In our fast-paced digital world, your virtual workspace can quickly become as cluttered as a desk piled high with papers. For adults with ADHD, this digital disorder can mirror the chaos of a physical room, leading to increased stress and decreased productivity. A tidy digital environment enhances efficiency and eases visual stress, allowing you to focus on what truly matters. Think of your computer desktop as the front page of your digital life. When it's clean and organized, it sets a positive tone, reducing the anxiety associated with the disorder. Just as a cluttered desk can distract you, a busy desktop filled with random icons and files can pull your attention in a thousand directions. By keeping it tidy, you clear mental space, making it easier to concentrate and get things done.

To set up an efficient digital workspace, customize your desktop layout for the best use possible. Arrange your most-used apps and files in a way that makes sense to you, placing them within easy reach. Consider using virtual backgrounds that are simple and free from distractions. A calming image can help reduce visual noise, allowing you to focus better on your tasks. This personalization creates an environment that feels welcoming and conducive to productivity. Next, organize your digital folders and files similarly to how you manage a filing cabinet. Create main folders for broad categories such as Travel, Hobbies, Writing, and Work. Then, create subfolders for specific topics within each category, such as "Travel to the Maldives in 2015," "Travel to Nepal," and "Travel to Singapore 2024." This organizational structure helps you quickly locate what you need, reducing the time spent searching through a digital maze. Consistent naming conventions for files ensure you always know where to look, making your workflow smoother and more efficient. Nothing is worse than a mix-up, a mismatch of file names. For instance, when you look for the latest file on Travel to Delhi, is it New Delhi 1.0, Deli A.0, or Delhi AA01?

Implementing a consistent file naming convention is a key strategy. By using clear, descriptive names, you can quickly identify documents without opening them. This consistency streamlines your workflow, reducing frustration and saving time.

Digital tools can significantly assist in maintaining an organized workspace. Productivity apps like Evernote or Notion can help you manage tasks and notes, keeping everything in one place. These tools offer features like tagging, reminders, and collaborative options, making them versatile for personal and professional use. Screen management tools are also invaluable, especially if you tend to multitask. They allow you to organize open windows, keeping your desktop neat and your focus sharp. Using these resources enhances your ability to manage digital clutter, much like organizing physical spaces in your home.

To keep your digital environment tidy over time, please set up a routine for clearing temporary files and downloads. Regularly review these areas, deleting unnecessary items and sorting essential items into appropriate folders. This practice prevents the buildup of digital clutter, ensuring your workspace remains clean and efficient. Maintaining an organized virtual workspace requires regular effort, but the benefits are substantial. With a tidy digital environment, you can focus more on your tasks and less on finding what you need.

The impact of an organized virtual workspace on productivity and mental clarity cannot be overstated. It mirrors the effects of a clutter-free home, providing a foundation for focused, practical work. By creating a space where everything has its place, you foster a sense of order and calm beyond the screen, enhancing your overall well-being.

7.3 Managing Digital Distractions and Notifications

In today's digital age, distractions lurk at every corner of your screen. The allure of social media and news alerts is particularly potent, pulling you away from tasks with their promise of instant information or entertainment. Each notification, whether from a buzzing phone or a blinking email icon, demands attention, yes, your attention, disrupting your focus and derailing productivity. For individuals with ADHD, these interruptions can be incredibly challenging to manage, leading to a fragmented attention span. The constant barrage of digital alerts not only chips away at your concentration but can also lead to increased stress and anxiety as you struggle to keep up with the relentless flow of information. It feels like you're caught in a cycle of perpetual distraction, where each beep or buzz adds to the mental clutter that already fills your day.

Practical strategies become your ally in combating numerous distractions. One helpful approach is setting specific times to check emails and social media. By allocating designated periods for these activities, you control when you engage with digital content rather than allowing it to dictate your day. This routine helps you stay focused on the task, knowing that you have scheduled time to catch up on messages later. Additionally, browser extensions can be a significant change, blocking access to websites that tend to pull you away from work. These tools create a barrier between you and digital temptations, allowing you to maintain your focus and accomplish more in less time.

Notification management is another crucial element in reducing digital distractions. Adjusting notification settings helps you manage which alerts are prioritized and which are silenced. This way, essential alerts will notify you only, helping you maintain focus without frequent interruptions. Enabling "Do Not Disturb" modes during focus periods is another effective way to minimize interruptions. This feature silences incoming alerts, creating a quiet environment where you can work without distraction. Implementing these strategies can significantly improve concentration, reducing the stress of managing a constant flow of digital information.

Please look at the story of a professional who drastically improved their workflow by limiting email access. Instead of keeping their email clients open all day, they scheduled specific times to check messages. This allowed them to focus on their primary tasks without the ping of incoming emails disrupting their flow. This change increased their productivity and reduced the anxiety associated with a constantly full inbox. Similarly, a student found that silencing phone notifications during study sessions enhanced their ability to concentrate. Turning off alerts created an environment conducive to deep focus, leading to more effective study sessions and better academic performance.

These examples highlight the transformative power of managing digital distractions. You create space for focused work and mental clarity by taking control of your digital environment. The constant pull of notifications and alerts no longer dictates your day, freeing you to engage more fully with the task. As you implement these strategies, you'll find the peace and productivity you gain worth the effort.

7.4 Streamlining Digital Files and Photos

Your computer and phone can become as cluttered as any physical space in your home. A virtual mess of untagged photos and disorganized documents can create as much stress as a pile of clothes or papers on the floor. As these digital files accumulate, they can lead to confusion and frustration, especially when trying to locate something crucial at the last minute. Organizing these elements is not just about creating order; it's about enhancing your ability to access what you need when you need it, thus preventing digital overload. Imagine scrolling endlessly through a sea of random, untagged photos to find that one picture from last summer, that one of you that makes you look cuter or younger! Try rifling through countless files with cryptic names to locate a crucial document. This scenario is all too common and can be incredibly time-consuming and stressful for anyone without ADHD, but combine this with ADHD, and WOW, do you have one nasty cocktail?

OK, so you have set up broad categories of folders and sub-folders, as mentioned earlier in the previous section. Refer to 7.4, Travel, which contains subfolders for the places visited by date; software such as Google Photos or Documents allows you to file the latest photos and documents as they come in, maintaining order from the start. If you frequently schedule time to go through your digital archives, deleting duplicates and outdated files that no longer serve a purpose. This practice trees up storage space and makes it easier to find what remains, reducing the mental clutter of navigating a disorganized digital landscape.

Several tools can make managing digital photos more efficient. Photo management software such as Google Photos or Adobe Lightroom offers features that can help you organize and store images easily. These apps allow you to tag and categorize photos, making it simple to locate them later. They also provide cloud storage solutions, ensuring your memories are safe and accessible from anywhere. Utilizing such tools allows you to transform a chaotic digital photo album into a streamlined collection, preserving your memories without the stress of disorganization.

The benefits of a streamlined digital archive extend beyond mere convenience. An organized digital collection enhances efficiency, allowing for the quick retrieval of important documents and cherished memories. This accessibility reduces the stress of searching for files, freeing up mental energy for more critical tasks. Additionally, a simplified digital environment contributes to peace of mind. Knowing everything is in its proper place provides a sense of control, reduces anxiety, and supports a more focused and productive mindset. With fewer digital distractions, you can direct your attention to what truly matters, enjoying the clarity and calmness of a well-organized virtual space.

Remember, just as the decluttering of real life, physical items, or space, whether furniture or clothes, needs to be reviewed frequently, it is an ongoing process. The same rules apply to your digital files and photos, so it's essential to schedule periodic check-ins to ensure your files remain organized and update systems to accommodate new files and evolving needs. Keeping up with these small tasks can prevent digital clutter from accumulating, preserving the order and serenity you've worked hard to create.

Streamlining digital files and photos is another significant step toward a clutter-free, serene environment. This effort enhances your day-to-day efficiency and contributes to your overall well-being, reinforcing the happiness of living with less. With a tidy digital space, you're better prepared to tackle the challenges of the physical world, knowing that your virtual life is in order. As you continue this journey towards organization and clarity, remember that each small step brings you closer to a life where clutter no longer holds sway, where calmness and serenity reign.

With visualization as a powerful ally, you're well-equipped to tackle decluttering challenges. As you progress, harness this clarity and motivation, letting it guide you toward a more organized and fulfilling life.

Chapter 7: Digital Decluttering for Mental Clarity

If you picture this, your phone buzzes, a notification lights up, and suddenly, you're pulled away from the task at hand, and your focus is lost instantly.

This cycle repeats, leaving you feeling scattered, all over the place, and overwhelmed. For adults with ADHD, the digital world can be particularly distracting, contributing to stress and reducing focus. However, it is very possible to regain control and clarity by embarking on a digital detox. This concept involves intentionally disconnecting from devices to refresh your mind and reduce stress.

Why is this necessary? In today's hyper-connected era, digital detoxes provide much-needed relief from the constant influx of information. They allow you to reset, helping you refocus on what truly matters. Just as clutter in your home can cause chaos, digital clutter can overwhelm your mental space, making it difficult to concentrate and function effectively.

Unplugging from the digital world helps you reclaim your mental health, allowing you to breathe and rediscover the joys of being present.

The benefits of unplugging are profound. When you step away from screens, you reduce exposure to the constant stimuli that can overtax your brain. This break allows your mind to rest, decreasing stress levels and improving overall mood. Without the distraction of notifications, you can engage more fully with the world around you, enhancing your relationships and boosting your productivity. Unplugging also helps reset your brain's dopamine levels, which can become overstimulated by endless digital interactions. This reset improves focus and concentration, paving the way for more meaningful and intentional engagement with technology when you return.

Setting boundaries for digital consumption, just as you would with children, is crucial in returning to what is real. You should, without a doubt, establish tech-free zones or times in your home when devices are banned. The dining room may become a no-phone zone; encouraging mealtime conversations after all sitting down together at mealtimes and communicating with each other is or should be something we all strive for. Or you can designate an hour before bed as screen-free, allowing your mind to wind down and prepare for restful sleep. These boundaries create a healthier relationship with technology, reminding you that not every moment needs to be filled with digital noise.

Instead, look at opportunities for offline activities, such as reading a book, walking, or enjoying a hobby or sport. These moments of disconnection foster creativity and mindfulness, enriching your life in ways that screens cannot.

Find alternative activities to fill the time traditionally spent online. It could be a new fitness routine, exploring nature, or spending quality time with loved ones. Engaging in these offline pursuits helps you reconnect with yourself and those around you, strengthening personal bonds and enhancing well-being.

The impact of digital clutter on mental health is significant. Constant emails and social media notifications create a perpetual state of alertness, making it difficult to relax and focus. This digital noise contributes to overwhelm and distractibility, particularly for individuals with ADHD. The pressure of being constantly "on" and available can lead to burnout, as your brain struggles to process the endless stream of information. Reducing digital interactions alleviates this electronic device stress, giving your mind the space to function optimally.

I don't know about anyone who has not gained from a digital detox. Success stories abound of individuals who have benefited from digital detox practices. Consider how one family that adopted weekly tech-free evenings discovered the joy of board games, storytelling, and deep conversations, strengthening their connections without the interference of screens. Another narrative involves a weekend retreat spent entirely offline. Participants reported feeling rejuvenated and more focused, with a renewed appreciation for the world around them. These experiences highlight the transformative power of stepping away from technology, if only temporarily.

Reflection Section: Planning Your Digital Detox,

Please look at your current relationship with technology. Are there areas where digital interactions feel overwhelming or intrusive? Set aside time to plan a digital detox. Identify tech-free zones or times and choose offline activities that bring you joy. Record your intentions in a journal, noting any anticipated challenges and how you plan to overcome them. Reflect on the potential benefits of this disconnection, envisioning the clarity and calm it might bring. Use this reflection to guide your digital detox, welcoming the peace and presence of stepping away from screens.

As you explore the idea of a digital detox, remember that it's not about eliminating technology. Instead, it's about creating a balanced relationship that enhances your life rather than detracting from it. Embrace the opportunity to reset and recharge, finding serenity in the space between the Beep and buzzing notifications!

7.2 Organizing Your Virtual Workspace

In our fast-paced digital world, your virtual workspace can quickly become as cluttered as a desk piled high with papers. For adults with ADHD, this digital disorder can mirror the chaos of a physical room, leading to increased stress and decreased productivity. A tidy digital environment enhances efficiency and eases visual stress, allowing you to focus on what truly matters. Think of your computer desktop as the front page of your digital life. When it's clean and organized, it sets a positive tone, reducing the anxiety associated with the disorder. Just as a cluttered desk can distract you, a busy desktop filled with random icons and files can pull your attention in a thousand directions. By keeping it tidy, you clear mental space, making it easier to concentrate and get things done.

To set up an efficient digital workspace, customize your desktop layout for the best use possible. Consistent naming conventions for files ensure you always know where to look, making your workflow smoother and more efficient. Implementing a consistent file naming convention is a key strategy. By using clear, descriptive names, you can quickly identify documents without opening them. This consistency streamlines your workflow, reducing frustration and saving time.

Digital tools can significantly assist in maintaining an organized workspace. Productivity apps like Evernote or Notion can help you manage tasks and notes, keeping everything in one place. These tools offer features like tagging, reminders, and collaborative options, making them versatile for personal and professional use. Screen management tools are also invaluable, especially if you tend to multitask. They allow you to organize open windows, keeping your desktop neat and your focus sharp. Using these resources enhances your ability to manage digital clutter, much like organizing physical spaces in your home.

To keep your digital environment tidy over time, please set up a routine for clearing temporary files and downloads. Regularly review these areas, deleting unnecessary items and sorting essential items into appropriate folders. This practice prevents the buildup of digital clutter, ensuring your workspace remains clean and efficient. Maintaining an organized virtual workspace requires regular effort, but the benefits are substantial. With a tidy digital environment, you can focus more on your tasks and less on finding what you need.

The impact of an organized virtual workspace on productivity and mental clarity cannot be overstated. It mirrors the effects of a clutter-free home, providing a foundation for focused, practical work. By creating a space where everything has its place, you foster a sense of order and calm beyond the screen, enhancing your overall well-being.

7.3 Managing Digital Distractions and Notifications

In today's digital age, distractions lurk at every corner of your screen. The allure of social media and news alerts is particularly potent, pulling you away from tasks with their promise of instant information or entertainment. Each notification, whether from a buzzing phone or a blinking email icon, demands attention, yes, your attention, disrupting your focus and derailing productivity. For individuals with ADHD, these interruptions can be incredibly challenging to manage, leading to a fragmented attention span. The constant barrage of digital alerts not only chips away at your concentration but can also lead to increased stress and anxiety as you struggle to keep up with the relentless flow of information. It feels like you're caught in a cycle of perpetual distraction, where each beep or buzz adds to the mental clutter that already fills your day.

Practical strategies become your ally in combating numerous distractions. One helpful approach is setting specific times to check emails and social media. By allocating designated periods for these activities, you control when you engage with digital content rather than allowing it to dictate your day. This routine helps you stay focused on the task, knowing that you have scheduled time to catch up on messages later. Additionally, browser extensions can be a momentous change, blocking access to websites that tend to pull you away from work. These tools create a barrier between you and digital temptations, allowing you to maintain your focus and accomplish more in less time.

Notification management is another crucial element in reducing digital distractions. By customizing your notification settings, you can prioritize essential alerts and silence those less critical ones. This means you'll only be interrupted by notifications that genuinely matter, allowing you to maintain concentration without constantly being pulled in different directions. Enabling "Do Not Disturb" modes during focus periods is another effective way to minimize interruptions. This feature silences incoming alerts, creating a quiet environment where you can work without distraction. Implementing these strategies can significantly improve concentration, reducing the stress of managing a constant flow of digital information.

The transformative power of managing digital distractions is that you create space for focused work and mental clarity by taking control of your digital environment. The constant pull of notifications and alerts no longer dictates your day, freeing you to engage more fully with the task. As you implement these strategies, you'll find the peace and productivity you gain worth the effort.

7.4 Streamlining Digital Files and Photos

Your computer and phone can become as cluttered as any physical space in your home. A virtual mess of untagged photos and disorganized documents can create as much stress as a pile of clothes or papers on the floor. As these digital files accumulate, they can lead to confusion and frustration, especially when trying to locate something crucial at the last minute. Organizing these elements is not just about creating order; it's about enhancing your ability to access what you need when you need it, thus preventing digital overload. Imagine scrolling endlessly through a sea of random, untagged photos to find that one picture from last summer, that one of you that makes you look cuter or younger! Try rifling through countless files with cryptic names to locate a crucial document. This scenario is all too common and can be incredibly time-consuming and stressful for anyone without ADHD, but combine this with ADHD, and WOW, do you have one nasty cocktail?

OK, so you have set up broad categories of folders and sub-folders, as mentioned earlier in the previous section. Refer to 7.4, Travel, which contains subfolders for the places visited by date; software such as Google Photos or Documents allows you to file the latest photos and documents as they come in, maintaining order from the start. If you frequently schedule time to go through your digital archives, deleting duplicates and outdated files that no longer serve a purpose. This practice frees up storage space and makes it easier to find what remains, reducing the mental clutter of navigating a disorganized digital landscape.

Several tools can make managing digital photos more efficient. Photo management software such as Google Photos or Adobe Lightroom offers features that can help you organize and store images easily. These apps allow you to tag and categorize photos, making it simple to locate them later. They also provide cloud storage solutions, ensuring your memories are safe and accessible from anywhere. Utilizing such tools allows you to transform a chaotic digital photo album into a streamlined collection, preserving your memories without the stress of disorganization.

The benefits of a streamlined digital archive extend beyond mere convenience. An organized digital collection enhances efficiency, allowing for the quick retrieval of important documents and cherished memories. This accessibility reduces the stress of searching for files, freeing up mental energy for more critical tasks. Additionally, a simplified digital environment contributes to peace of mind. Knowing everything is in its proper place provides a sense of control, reduces anxiety, and supports a more focused and productive mindset. With fewer digital distractions, you can direct your attention to what truly matters, enjoying the clarity and calmness of a well-organized virtual space.

Remember, just as the decluttering of real life, physical items, or space, whether furniture or clothes, needs to be reviewed frequently, it is an ongoing process. The same rules apply to your digital files and photos, so it's essential to schedule periodic check-ins to ensure your files remain organized and update systems to accommodate new files and evolving needs. Keeping up with these small tasks can prevent digital clutter from accumulating, preserving the order and serenity you've worked hard to create.

Streamlining digital files and photos is another significant step toward a clutter-free, serene environment. This effort enhances your day-to-day efficiency and contributes to your overall well-being, reinforcing the happiness of living with less. With a tidy digital space, you're better prepared to tackle the challenges of the physical world, knowing that your virtual life is in order. As you continue this journey towards organization and clarity, remember that each small step brings you closer to a life where clutter no longer holds sway, where calmness and serenity reign.

Chapter 8: Mindful Living and Minimalism

"The first step in crafting the life you want is eliminating everything you don't."
— Joshua Becker

Can you already feel a profound sense of tranquility? The space breathes with openness, each item thoughtfully chosen and cherished. This is the essence of minimalism—a lifestyle that champions simplicity and intentionality. For adults with ADHD, the constant barrage of stimuli can be overwhelming. Minimalism offers a sanctuary from this chaos, a way to reduce distractions and focus on what truly matters. At its core, minimalism is about quality over quantity, valuing experiences over possessions. It's about shifting your mindset to prioritize what enriches your life rather than merely filling it.

Adopting a minimalist mindset begins with questioning the necessity of each new purchase. In a world driven by consumerism, it's easy to accumulate without much thought. But ask yourself: Does this item add value to my life? Will it bring any quantity of joy or serve a purpose? Embracing having "enough" is a powerful tool against the urge to acquire more, mindlessly purchasing additional items that have no value in one's life. It's about recognizing when you have what you need and resisting the pull of excess. This shift in thinking helps combat clutter and fosters a sense of contentment and gratitude for what you already possess. It is, without a doubt, a profound way of living your life.

The psychological benefits of minimalism are profound. By minimizing clutter, you reduce the mental burden of decision-making and the constant visual noise that can distract and overwhelm you. Minimalism creates a calm space where the focus can thrive. Testimonials from minimalists often speak to the joy found in simplicity. Laura, who has ADHD, shares that minimalism has helped her by giving everything a place, reducing the mental load of clutter that once clouded her mind (SOURCE 1). You cultivate an environment that supports mental clarity and well-being by creating a space that reflects your needs and values.

Real-life stories of minimalist transformations offer inspiration and insight. Consider a family that decided to downsize, focusing on experiences rather than possessions. They found that living with less gave them more time and energy to invest in activities that brought them joy. Their weekends were no longer consumed by cleaning and organizing. Instead, they spent time outdoors, traveling, and connecting with loved ones. This shift strengthened their family bonds and enriched their lives with memories and meaning that material goods would never be able to do.

Another compelling narrative is that of a professional who simplified their life to boost productivity. By decluttering their workspace and home, they eliminated distractions that once hindered their focus. The newfound clarity allowed them to streamline their daily routines, increasing efficiency and reducing stress. This minimalist approach extended beyond physical space, influencing their professional and personal decisions. By prioritizing what mattered, they achieved a harmonious balance that enhanced their career and personal fulfillment.

Minimalism is not just about decluttering physical spaces; it's a mindset that permeates every aspect of life. It encourages intentional decision-making, focusing on what aligns with your goals and values. By embracing minimalism, you create an organized and deeply fulfilling life. The happiness of less becomes a lived reality that empowers you to focus on the richness of experiences and the serenity of a clutter-free life.

Reflection Section: Embracing Minimalism

Take a moment to reflect on your own life. Are there areas where you feel overwhelmed by possessions? Consider conducting a "minimalism audit." Identify items that hold value and those that contribute to clutter. Write down your findings and assess what changes you can make to embrace a minimalist lifestyle. This exercise is not about immediate transformation but small, meaningful steps toward simplicity and serenity.

8.2 The Art of Mindful Living in Daily Routines

Mindful living is about being truly present in each moment, savoring the here and now without distraction or judgment. In a world of noise, mindfulness invites us to slow down and engage fully with our surroundings. It transforms everyday activities into opportunities for reflection and appreciation. Imagine starting your day not with a rushed breakfast but with a quiet moment of gratitude for the meal before you. This simple shift can foster a deeper connection to your daily experiences, helping you see beauty in the mundane. Practicing gratitude for life's small pleasures can create a ripple effect of positivity, enhancing your overall sense of well-being and contentment.

Incorporating mindfulness into daily routines can be both simple and rewarding. Take mindful eating, for instance. Instead of multitasking during meals, try focusing solely on eating. Notice the flavors, textures, and aromas of each bite. This practice enhances your dining experience and encourages healthier eating habits as you're more attuned to your body's hunger and fullness signals. Similarly, mindful walking invites you to connect with your environment. As you walk, pay attention to the sensation of your feet touching the ground, the rhythm of your breath, and the sights and sounds around you. This practice can be particularly grounding, offering a sense of peace and clarity amidst the chaos of life.

The benefits of mindfulness extend beyond immediate experience. Mindfulness can improve focus and reduce mental clutter by cultivating awareness and intentionality. Mindful breathing exercises, for instance, have a calming effect on the mind and body. Take a few moments each day to practice deep, intentional breathing, which can help reduce stress and anxiety and enhance your ability to concentrate on the tasks. Research has shown that mindfulness practices can significantly reduce anxiety and boost well-being (SOURCE 2). This is especially relevant for individuals with ADHD, where the constant mental chatter can feel overwhelming. Integrating mindfulness into your routine creates space for clarity and calm, making it easier to navigate daily challenges.

Consider the story of a parent who embraced mindful parenting to strengthen family bonds. By being fully present with their children, they could engage more meaningfully, fostering connections built on understanding and empathy. This shift deepened their relationship and created a more harmonious home environment. Another example is an employee who uses mindfulness to manage workplace stress. They became more focused and less reactive by incorporating brief meditation sessions into their day, increasing productivity and job satisfaction. These stories highlight the transformative power of mindfulness in everyday life, illustrating how minor changes can lead to profound improvements in mental clarity and emotional resilience.

Amid life's demands, mindfulness offers a refuge—a way to ground yourself in the present and appreciate the richness of each moment. By embracing mindful living, you cultivate a deeper connection to yourself and the world. This practice invites you to slow down, breathe deeply, and savor life's simple joys. Whether through mindful eating, walking, or breathing, these practices encourage a shift from mindless activity to meaningful engagement. Doing so opens the door to a life filled with greater awareness, contentment, and serenity.

8.3 Creating a Calm and Centred Home Environment

Picture your home as a sanctuary, a refuge from the outside world's chaos. For adults with ADHD, a calm and organized home environment is more than just pleasant. It's vital. A serene space can significantly reduce stress, providing a healthy foundation for mindfulness and minimalism. The physical environment profoundly impacts mood and focus, and cluttered or chaotic spaces often reflect and reinforce mental clutter. When your home is peaceful, thinking, making decisions, and finding balance becomes more effortless.

Designing a calming home atmosphere involves thoughtful choices that prioritize tranquility. Natural elements like plants and water features bring life and freshness into a room, creating a soothing ambiance. Plants purify the air and introduce a touch of nature, connecting you with the outdoors. A small fountain or fish tank can add a gentle sound of water, enhancing relaxation and reducing stress. Selecting calming colors is another step toward a peaceful home. Soft blues, greens, and neutral tones promote relaxation and peace. Textures also play a role—opt for soft fabrics and materials that invite touch and comfort. For example, velvets and faux furs transform your space into a haven of serenity.

Incorporating feng shui principles can enhance your home's energy flow and balance. This ancient Chinese practice focuses on harmonizing the environment, promoting well-being and positive energy. Arranging furniture to facilitate movement and conversation is key. Avoid blocking pathways with bulky furniture, as clear paths allow energy to flow freely. Decluttering entrances are significant; a welcoming hallway invites opportunities and positive experiences into your life. Please look at the furniture and decor to ensure each room supports its intended function: ask yourself if it is suited to the planned activity, relaxation, work, or socializing.

Take inspiration from real-life transformations. A couple decided to redesign their living room, aiming to create a space dedicated to relaxation. They removed unnecessary furniture, painting the walls a calming shade of sage green. A soft area rug and comfortable seating encouraged lounging and conversation. The result was an open and inviting living room, a perfect retreat for unwinding after a long day. Another example is a student who optimized their study area for concentration. They created a focused, productive environment that minimized distractions by decluttering their desk and incorporating calming elements like a small plant and a warm desk lamp.

Your home environment can profoundly impact on your well-being. A calm, centered space supports your efforts to live mindfully and embrace minimalism. It becomes a place where you can recharge, reflect, and find peace amidst the demands of daily life. Creating such an environment requires intention and reflection, but the rewards are immense. By prioritizing tranquility in your home, you nurture a space that supports your goals and enhances your quality of life.

8.4 Balancing Simplicity with Practical Needs

Striking a balance between simplicity and practicality is the heart of a minimalist lifestyle without compromising functionality. It's about ensuring that simplicity enhances your life rather than stripping it of comfort and efficiency. Start by identifying the essentials for daily living, which means recognizing what you truly need and using it regularly. Walk through your home and consider each item: does it serve a purpose? Is it used often? By focusing on essentials, you can streamline your possessions, making space for what truly matters.

In your quest for balance, prioritize multipurpose items. Imagine a sofa bed that is a comfortable couch by day and a guest bed by night. This dual functionality saves space and resources. Similarly, a dining table that doubles as a workspace is another example of how to maximize utility. Choosing items with more than one use reduces clutter and invites a sense of spaciousness into your environment. It's about making thoughtful choices that support both form and function.

Maintaining this balance requires regular assessment of your possessions. Please set aside time periodically to look over your items, assessing each for necessity and value. This habit keeps your space from becoming overwhelmed with non-essentials. Implementing a "one in, one out" policy can also help maintain equilibrium. Consider parting with something else when introducing the latest item into your home. This practice prevents the slow creep of clutter and ensures that your living space remains intentional and organized.

Balancing simplicity with practicality offers numerous benefits, including reduced decision fatigue. With fewer items, everyday decisions become more manageable and quicker. You'll spend less time searching for items or deciding what to wear. This clarity frees up mental energy, allowing you to focus on meaningful activities and experiences. It also creates a more peaceful environment, where everything has its place and chaos is minimized.

Today is the day you rid yourself of anything distracting from your best life."

— Joshua Becker, The Minimalist Home

Consider stories of individuals who have successfully harmonized minimalism with practicality. A chef, for example, streamlined their kitchen by focusing on essential tools and appliances. By eliminating duplicates and unused gadgets, they created a space where cooking became a joy rather than a chore. The efficiency gained allowed them to experiment with new recipes and techniques, enhancing their culinary creativity. In another narrative, a traveler embraced minimalism to ease the planning of frequent journeys. They quickly and gracefully moved through airports and cities by curating a versatile wardrobe and minimizing luggage. This approach simplified their travels and enriched their experiences, as they could focus on the journey rather than the baggage.

Through these examples, it's clear that balancing simplicity with practicality is achievable and deeply rewarding. It leads to a life where clarity and convenience coexist, and your environment supports your goals and values. This balance is key to living a functional, fulfilling, minimalist lifestyle.

Chapter 8 has explored how minimalism and mindfulness can transform your living space and daily routines, merging simplicity with practicality. The next chapter will address common decluttering challenges and offer solutions to maintain a clutter-free life.

Chapter 9: Overcoming Common Decluttering Challenges

Imagine walking into your home, eager to breathe life into your shared spaces. Yet, each room tells a different story, as family members' belongings intertwine, creating a patchwork of personalities and memories. For adults with ADHD, this complexity can feel particularly overwhelming. Navigating the labyrinth of family dynamics and shared spaces is both a challenge and an opportunity. The living room, kitchen, and bathroom become battlegrounds where clutter often wins. Each person's definition of what needs to stay or go may differ, creating tension and stalling progress. Balancing individual and collective needs require physical sorting and emotional negotiation. It's about finding harmony in diversity, where everyone's voice is heard, and no one's belongings dominate the space.

Effective communication is at the heart of overcoming these challenges. It's essential to foster an environment where open discussions can occur, allowing family members to express their needs and concerns without fear of judgment. Setting family meetings to discuss decluttering goals can be a powerful tool. Use these gatherings to establish clear rules and responsibilities for each shared space. For instance, designate areas for communal use and others for personal belongings. Define what clutter means to each family member, acknowledging that perceptions vary widely. This collaborative approach eases tension and empowers everyone to take ownership of their environment.

To accommodate diverse preferences, consider creating personalized zones within shared areas. In the living room, for example, allocate specific corners for each family member's hobbies or interests. These zones allow individuals to maintain a sense of personal space within the communal area, reducing friction over clutter. Encourage each family member to have a say in decluttering, ensuring that decisions reflect the collective vision rather than a single perspective. This inclusivity fosters a sense of belonging and respect, strengthening family bonds while maintaining order.

Consider the story of the Johnson family, who effectively transformed their living room into a functional, shared space. Each member had unique needs—Dad enjoyed reading, Mom loved crafting, and the kids needed a play area. By designating specific zones for each activity, they preserved individual interests while keeping the room tidy. Shelves housed Dad's books, a corner became Mom's crafting nook with organized supplies, and a play area was established with labeled toy bins. This arrangement reduced clutter and encouraged everyone to respect and maintain their designated space. The living room became a harmonious blend of personal expression and communal living, enhancing the family's daily interactions.

In the same way, consider a couple who approached their bedroom organization with compromise. Both partners had differing views on what constituted clutter. They reached a solution that suited both by openly discussing their needs and preferences. They agreed to organize the closet with clear divisions for each person's clothing. The dresser had designated drawers for shared items like linens, while individual drawers held personal belongings. This compromise respected each partner's definition of clutter, creating a peaceful and organized bedroom. Their willingness to communicate and adapt resulted in a space that supported both individuals' comfort and well-being.

Creating a shared space accommodating everyone's needs requires patience, empathy, and flexibility. It's about recognizing that clutter is physical, emotional, and relational. Only through open communication, collaboration, and compromise can challenges turn into opportunities for growth and compromise. As you embark on this journey, remember that each family member's perspective is equally valid. By working together, you can create an environment that reflects the uniqueness of each individual while fostering a sense of unity and tranquility.

9.2 Handling Setbacks and Plateaus

Picture the excitement of embarking on a decluttering mission fueled by the promise of a tidy and serene space. Yet, as you dive deeper into the process, you might find yourself stuck, and your motivation has hit that brick wall, leaving you at an all-time low. The initial burst of enthusiasm has fizzled out, giving way to feelings of overwhelm, stagnation, and paralysis. Tackling a project too large can quickly lead to a sense of defeat. You might start with ambitious plans to overhaul an entire room, only to find yourself buried under piles of items with no clear path forward. This is a common setback—biting off more than you can chew. Oh yes, that old chestnut! Without visible progress, motivation can dwindle, leaving you questioning whether your efforts are worthwhile.

Just as every other action needs to be frequently adjusted and tweaked, it is critical to reassess and change your approach to overcome these plateaus. Revisiting your decluttering plans can give you the clarity needed to reignite momentum. Break down overwhelming tasks into more manageable steps. Instead of "cleaning the entire double garage," focus on "organizing the tool shelf" or "sorting through gardening supplies." Tackling these bite-sized pieces offers immediate gratification, restoring that sense of accomplishment that again motivates further action. This reduces the feeling of being overwhelmed and makes the process less daunting. A practical strategy is to set specific, achievable goals for each decluttering session. Please remember the 15-minute decluttering sessions. These achievable objectives help maintain calm and serenity.

Fifteen minutes daily is not much to pay to keep your motivation alive and maintain calm and serenity! Today, focus solely on clearing one small drawer or organizing a single shelf. These small victories accumulate, gradually transforming your space.

Maintaining a positive mindset is essential, as optimism and resilience are potent allies in overcoming obstacles. Celebrate your small victories; 15 minutes a day is an achievable goal. Each item sorted, each drawer cleared, is a step toward your goal. Treat yourself kindly, practicing self-compassion and patience. Understand that setbacks are likely to happen and are natural, not failures, but opportunities to learn and adapt. By embracing these moments, you cultivate resilience, which fortifies you against future challenges.

Please know that decluttering is a journey that requires time, effort, and persistence. It's not a one-time job.

I have practiced 15 minutes a day to declutter. When I found myself at a standstill, my initial enthusiasm waning as I faced that brick wall, I became very aware that if I changed tactics, I would reignite my progress. Instead of decluttering an entire room, I created "quick wins." I set a timer for 15 minutes each day, dedicating that time to clearing a small area. This strategy shift broke the plateau and restored my motivation, as each completed task fueled the desire to continue.

Others found renewed motivation through community support. Feeling stuck, they contacted a local decluttering group, where members shared their experiences and strategies. Through weekly meetups and shared goals, they found the encouragement needed to push past their plateau. The camaraderie and accountability offered by the group provided the boost they needed to keep going. This experience highlights the power of community in overcoming setbacks, proving that sometimes, the support of others can be the key to finding your way forward, and sometimes the opposite is true!

In the face of setbacks and plateaus, remember that progress is not always linear. Be patient with yourself, and have the grace to pause, reassess, and adapt. With determination, flexibility, and a positive mindset, you can overcome these challenges and continue moving toward a clutter-free, serene environment where the Happiness of Less is indeed experienced.

9.3 Addressing Fear of Discarding Important Items

The fear of accidentally discarding valuable items is a common hurdle in decluttering, especially for those who find emotional solace in their possessions. This anxiety often stems from the concern that something irreplaceable, like a cherished family photo or an important document, might be mistakenly thrown away. The thought of losing these items can induce significant stress, creating a mental block that prevents progress. The emotional weight of potential regret then adds to and compounds this anxiety. You may be paralyzed by the "what ifs," fearing that letting go of certain items could erase memories or disconnect you from your past. This fear is deeply rooted and can be challenging to overcome. However, you can confidently and readily navigate this emotional terrain by implementing thoughtful strategies.

To differentiate between essential and non-essential possessions, create a key list for evaluating an item's importance. Ask yourself: Does this item serve a practical purpose in my life today? Does it hold significant sentimental value beyond being a reminder of the past? These questions can help you assess whether an object is valuable or occupies space. Conducting a thorough review of sentimental value versus practical use can also enlighten. An item was once meaningful, but now it serves no actual function or emotional significance. Recognizing this shift allows you to let go without guilt, understanding its purpose has been fulfilled.

You can set up safety nets within your decluttering process to ease the fear of losing essential items. Secure storage solutions are invaluable for safeguarding key documents and items. Consider investing in a fireproof safe or a dedicated filing system to organize vital papers. Digitizing documents and photos are another effective strategy. Creating digital backups ensures these items are preserved, even if the originals are misplaced or damaged. This frees up physical space and allows you to enjoy a clutter-free environment without worrying about losing something valuable.

Please look at the story of a professional who successfully managed their fear of discarding essential work files. They implemented a robust backup system, storing digital copies on an external hard drive and a cloud service. This dual approach ensured their documents were always accessible, regardless of physical location. This strategy allowed them to confidently declutter their office, removing unnecessary paper clutter without worrying about losing critical information. Similarly, a parent preserved family photos through digital archiving. Scanning and organizing images into digital albums protected these memories from physical damage and made them easily shareable with family members. This approach transformed their fear of loss into a celebration of preservation, highlighting the joy of reliving memories in a new, accessible format.

Navigating the fear of discarding essential items requires patience and a willingness to embrace new preservation methods. By implementing these strategies, you can confidently approach decluttering with the assurance that your most valuable possessions are secure. This reduces anxiety and empowers you to let go of what no longer serves you, creating space for new experiences and memories. But seriously, do not shop for the latest items to fill the now-clear, clutter-free areas! As you move forward, remember that the goal is not to hold onto everything but to cherish and preserve what truly matters: the key cherished items.

9.4 Strategies for Consistency and Habit Formation

Building consistency in decluttering is like nurturing a plant; it requires regular attention and care, or it will die. For adults with ADHD, integrating decluttering into daily or weekly routines can transform it from a daunting task into a manageable habit. It's the habit you want to form; think of decluttering as part of your self-care routine, like brushing your teeth or walking. Establishing these routines prevents clutter from sneaking back into your life, ensuring that the calm and order you've worked hard to achieve remain intact. Begin by carving out small pockets of time each day dedicated to tidying up—as simple as sorting through mail right after lunch or spending a few minutes in the evening organizing your workspace. When done regularly, these small acts create a rhythm that keeps your environment tidy and reinforces a sense of control and accomplishment.

Forming and maintaining decluttering habits requires deliberate effort and the right tools. Habit trackers can be a powerful ally in this endeavor. By marking off each day, you engage in decluttering; you create a visual record of your progress, which can be highly motivating. Seeing a completed day chain can encourage you to keep going, transforming decluttering from an obligation into a gratifying routine. Reminders, whether digital or physical, also play a crucial role. A simple phone alert or a sticky note on your fridge can prompt you to dedicate those precious few minutes to tidying up. Start with small, consistent actions to build momentum. Let's begin with a single drawer or a small room section. As these actions become second nature, you'll naturally expand your efforts, gradually tackling larger projects with the same ease.

Accountability can significantly bolster the formation of new habits. Sharing your goals with a decluttering buddy or joining a group can provide the support and encouragement needed to stay on track. Regular check-ins, whether through phone calls or in-person meetups, create a sense of responsibility that can help sustain your decluttering efforts. Knowing that someone else is invested in your progress can be a powerful motivator, pushing you to maintain your routines even on days when motivation wanes. This shared journey fosters a sense of community, reminding you that you're not alone in your quest for a clutter-free life.

Please look at the story of a student who successfully integrated decluttering into their study routine. Each time they sat down to study, they spent five minutes organizing their desk. This simple habit ensured that their workspace remained transparent and conducive to focus. Over time, these brief sessions expanded into organizing other areas of their room, creating a serene environment supporting academic and personal growth. Similarly, a retiree found peace by decluttering part of their morning ritual. After enjoying their morning coffee daily, they spent a few minutes tidying up a specific area of their home. This routine kept their space orderly and provided a sense of purpose and accomplishment, setting a positive tone for the rest of the day. Consistency is key. With regular practice, decluttering becomes less of a chore and more of a lifestyle. These small, consistent efforts accumulate, leading to sustainable results that prevent re-cluttering and maintain the serenity you've worked hard to achieve. By integrating decluttering into your daily life and leveraging tools and community support, you pave the way for lasting change.

Chapter 10: Utilizing Visual Aids and Interactive Tools

Just close your eyes and imagine walking into a cluttered room and feeling your mind immediately settles as you glance at a simple chart on the wall. The chaos fades, replaced by a clear plan that directs your actions. For adults with ADHD, the power of visual aids lies in their ability to transform overwhelming tasks into manageable steps. Visual cues—charts, diagrams, or lists—anchor you in the present and guide your focus. These tools tap into the brain's preference for visual information, converting abstract ideas into tangible forms that are easier to process and act upon. As a result, visual aids reduce the cognitive overload that often accompanies decluttering, allowing you to approach the task with clarity and confidence.

Visual aids can enhance cognitive processing by externalizing information, effectively supporting your thinking and decision-making processes. They bridge your intentions and actions, helping you maintain attention and follow through on your plans. Imagine using a color-coded chart to categorize items in your home. The colors provide a quick reference, reducing the time spent deliberating whether to keep, toss, donate, or recycle. This method simplifies complex tasks, breaking them down into smaller, more digestible parts. Using visual aids to outline your decluttering plans, you create a roadmap that guides you step-by-step, minimizing the mental strain of decision-making. It is one method you can utilize to keep you on track, remind you of your priorities, and celebrate as you meet each objective.

Charts offer a visual framework that streamlines, for example, the sorting process, making it more efficient and less daunting. Mind maps are another powerful tool, allowing you to outline decluttering plans and steps in a way that visually represents your thought process. They encourage you to explore different approaches and solutions, fostering creativity and flexibility in decluttering efforts. By mapping out your ideas, you gain a clearer understanding of the task at hand, making it easier to act and adapt as needed. Personalizing your visual aids ensures they resonate with your individual preferences and needs. If you find specific colors calming or energizing, incorporate them into your visual tools to enhance their effectiveness. This personalizing process inspires and motivates you to stay engaged.

For individuals with ADHD, visual aids offer distinct advantages by reducing distractions and enhancing clarity. They provide a structured way to approach tasks, minimizing the chaos that often accompanies decluttering. By simplifying complex tasks through visual breakdown, these tools help you focus one step at a time, reducing overwhelm that usually leads to procrastination. Visual repetition also reinforces memory, ensuring critical information stays at the top of the mind. This is particularly beneficial for those who struggle with working memory, as visual aids provide a constant reminder of your goals and priorities. Integrating these tools into your decluttering routine creates an environment that supports focus, clarity, and effective decision-making. The role of visual aids in this decluttering journey cannot be overstated. They transform an overwhelming process into a series of manageable steps, empowering you to take control of your space and your life. As you explore different visual aids and personalize them to suit your needs, you'll find that the path to a clutter-free, serene environment becomes more precise and more attainable.

Visual Exercise: Creating Your Personalized Visual Aid

Consider creating a personalized visual aid that reflects your decluttering goals. Start by identifying the areas you want to focus on and assigning colors to each category—green for items to keep, blue for donations, and red for discards. Use symbols or icons to represent different tasks or milestones. Once your visual aid is complete, please place it in a prominent location that can be a constant reminder and motivator. This exercise organizes your tasks and transforms your decluttering plan into a visual journey toward clarity and calmness.

Interactive Exercises for Sustained Interest

Imagine approaching decluttering with the same enthusiasm you would have for a favorite game. Interactive exercises offer this possibility, transforming a mundane task into something engaging and enjoyable. By actively participating in the process, you're not just checking off tasks; you're fully immersed, which enhances learning and retention. When decluttering becomes interactive, it breaks the monotony and injects fun and creativity. This is particularly beneficial for those with ADHD, where maintaining interest can often be a challenge. Active involvement keeps the mind engaged, making the process not only more effective but also more satisfying.

Could you create a decluttering bingo game? Each square on the bingo card represents a specific decluttering task, such as organizing a kitchen drawer or clearing a particular shelf. As you complete each task, could you mark off the square? The goal is to achieve bingo by completing a row, column, or diagonal function. This game-like structure offers a clear objective and a sense of accomplishment with each completed square. Alternatively, you might design a scavenger or treasure hunt to locate and declutter specific items throughout your home. This exercise turns decluttering into a treasure hunt, where each found item brings you closer to a more organized space. Surprise and discovery make the process exciting, encouraging continued participation.

Incorporating gamification into decluttering can significantly boost motivation. Setting up point systems for completed tasks creates a tangible measure of your progress. Each task earns points, and these points can accumulate toward a reward. After reaching specific points, you treat yourself to a favorite activity or a small indulgence. This system reinforces positive behavior and provides an additional incentive to continue decluttering. Small rewards for reaching milestones further enhance this motivational structure. Whether enjoying a special dessert after finishing a particularly challenging area or relaxing after a successful decluttering session, these rewards celebrate your efforts and motivate you.

The success of interactive exercises in decluttering is evident in the stories of those who've embraced these techniques. One family used a chore wheel to assign decluttering tasks, turning a potentially contentious activity into a collaborative effort. Each family member spun the wheel to determine their task, adding an element of chance and fairness to the process. This approach not only distributed the workload but also fostered a sense of teamwork and shared responsibility. In another instance, friends held a decluttering challenge with prizes for the most progress. This competitive aspect spurred participants to push themselves further while enjoying the camaraderie of friendly competition.

These examples highlight how interactive exercises encourage active participation, sustain interest, and provide a framework for motivation that can make a significant difference, especially for those with ADHD who may struggle with traditional methods. By tapping into the elements of play and reward, these exercises turn decluttering into an experience that is productive but also rewarding and fun.

10.2 Creating Visual Reminders for Motivation

Imagine walking through your home, and each space whispers encouragement, reminding you of your goals. Visual reminders do just that. They are not just decorations but powerful motivators that keep your decluttering efforts alive and vibrant. Something clicks in your mind when you see a motivational poster or sticky note with a simple reminder. It's as if these visuals reinforce your intentions, nudging you gently back on track whenever you feel your resolve waver. The psychological boost from seeing your accomplishments or the goals you've set for yourself creates a positive feedback loop. It's that slight push you need on days when motivation feels distant.

Creating effective visual reminders is an art. Start by crafting motivational posters that resonate with you. Choose quotes or affirmations that inspire action and positivity. See my concluding chapter for more affirmations, quotes, and such, including a humorous look at decluttering per se. Let's remind ourselves by boldly writing these words of inspiration and pearls of wisdom and placing them where you'll see them often. Sticky notes make excellent reminders. They're versatile, easy to move, and can carry those quick, encouraging nudges you need throughout the day. Think of them as mini cheerleaders scattered around to keep you focused. A note that says, "You've got this!" in your bathroom mirror can be just the lift you need in the morning.

The strategic placement of these reminders is crucial. Clutter hotspots are prime locations. Your targets are the kitchen counter, the entry hallway table, or the chair in your bedroom where you collect clothes. Position your motivational visuals in high-traffic areas where they'll catch your eye. The fridge is an excellent spot for a motivational poster because who doesn't visit it multiple times daily? By placing these cues in areas you frequent, you ensure they're not just seen but noticed, making their message integral to your daily routine.

Could you review the story of a teacher who used a vision board to track their decluttering goals? Each image and word on that board was a step towards a more organized life. It wasn't about dreaming but seeing those dreams daily and being reminded to act on them. Or think of the professional who displayed a progress chart in their office. Each time they looked at it, they saw tasks and victories. That chart wasn't just an indicator of progress but a testament to their commitment and capability. These stories highlight the effectiveness of visual reminders in keeping motivation alive and thriving.

Visual reminders serve as allies in your decluttering efforts. They capture your goals and intentions and turn them into companions, encouraging action and perseverance. With each glance, these visuals reaffirm your commitment, making the path to an organized space less daunting and more attainable. As you integrate visual reminders into your routine, you'll find that they don't just keep you on track; they celebrate your progress and inspire you to continue striving for the Happiness of less.

10.3 Digital Tools for Tracking Progress

In the whirlwind of daily life, keeping track of decluttering achievements can sometimes feel like an additional task on an overflowing to-do list. This is where digital tools step in as allies, offering a convenient way to monitor your progress and maintain momentum. Technology is a reliable partner, especially when juggling multiple responsibilities. Visualizing your accomplishments through charts and graphs allows you to transform abstract goals into concrete, visible results. Seeing your progress in such a tangible form reinforces your efforts and clearly shows how far you've come and how much further you can go.

The convenience of digital tracking is undeniable. For those constantly on the move, apps like Habitica or Streaks can be a game changer quite literally apps to gamify and reward good habits. These habit-tracking apps let you set goals, track your progress, and even reward yourself for completing tasks. They turn your decluttering process into a series of achievable milestones, keeping you motivated and focused. There is also the app "Brain.fm," which is music, especially for those with ADHD. It claims to be able to play music to encourage the ability to focus. Well, that is a no-brainer, then, for sure. Excuse the pun! Digital planners also play a crucial role, with features that allow you to set reminders and organize your tasks. They provide a structured space to outline your decluttering plan, ensuring nothing slips through the cracks. With these tools, you can plan your day precisely, knowing that your digital assistant keeps you on track.

Choosing the right digital tools requires carefully considering your preferences and needs. You can start by evaluating the user interface of each tool. It should be intuitive, requiring minimal effort to navigate and use. A cluttered or complicated app defeats the purpose of streamlining your tasks. Also, consider compatibility with your devices. Whether you use a smartphone, tablet, or computer, the tool should synchronize seamlessly across all platforms. This ensures that you can access your plans and progress no matter where you are. The right tool feels like an extension of yourself, seamlessly integrating into your routine without adding complexity.

For individuals with ADHD, digital tracking offers specific benefits that cater to their needs. Structure and accountability are key elements that these tools provide. Setting alerts and notifications prompts you to act, turning intentions into reality. These reminders serve as gentle nudges, helping you stay on top of your goals even when distractions threaten to derail your efforts. Moreover, these apps allow you to analyze data, identify patterns, and make informed adjustments to your strategy. By understanding what works and does not, you can refine your approach, ensuring that your efforts produce tangible results.

The power of digital tools lies in their ability to track progress and their capacity to transform the decluttering process into a more manageable and rewarding experience.

Technology becomes your partner, showing you each step forward. As you embrace these digital helpers, the clutter that once seemed daunting begins to diminish, replaced by an environment that supports your goals and well-being. The next chapter will explore how building a supportive community can further enhance and sustain your decluttering efforts.

Chapter 11: Building a Supportive Community

Imagine waking up, reaching for your phone, and feeling inspired as you scroll through a vibrant online community filled with stories of transformation. This community isn't about sharing pictures of immaculate spaces; it's a supportive hub for people like you, navigating the complexities of decluttering, especially with ADHD. The beauty of online groups lies in their accessibility, offering a vast array of perspectives and strategies that can illuminate your path to a clutter-free life. As you connect with others, you'll find that shared experiences create a sense of camaraderie and motivation, reminding you that you're not alone on this journey. Online decluttering communities bring together individuals from diverse backgrounds, offering unique insights. You might come across someone who has mastered organizing their kitchen while another has tackled their overflowing wardrobe with finesse. These groups provide a platform to share your challenges and receive empathetic advice. It's a space where victories are celebrated, no matter how small, and setbacks are met with understanding and encouragement. Engaging with these communities can transform your decluttering approach, offering practical solutions and emotional support. The collective wisdom found in these groups can be a meaningful change, providing tools and strategies you might not have considered on your own.

Finding the right online group that aligns with your goals and values. You can begin by evaluating the group's rules and culture. Is the environment positive and supportive? Do the members encourage each other with kindness and respect? An engaged and active group often has regular posts and interactions, fostering a dynamic and lively atmosphere. When looking at a group, please consider how the members communicate and whether their approach resonates with you. This alignment ensures that your time spent in the group is both productive and uplifting.

Popular platforms like Facebook and Reddit host many decluttering groups, each with a focus and community vibe. You might find a group dedicated to minimalist living or a forum inspired by Marie Kondo's philosophy. These spaces offer a treasure trove of resources, from practical tips to motivational stories. Exploring a few diverse groups can help you locate the right one. Whether you're drawn to a large, bustling community or a smaller, more intimate group, there's a space out there where you'll feel at home.

One powerful aspect of these online communities is the opportunity to partner with an accountability buddy. Pairing up with someone with similar goals can enhance your commitment and provide a sense of shared responsibility. Regular check-ins, whether through video calls or messaging, create a structure that keeps you on track. Sharing weekly goals and progress updates with your partner holds you accountable and allows you to celebrate each other's successes. This mutual support forms a bond that can motivate and comfort, making the decluttering process less daunting. It's interesting how perspectives on accountability partners can vary widely. While some argue that having someone to share goals with can keep you motivated and on track, others caution that it might lead to pressure or even a fear of failure. The saying you're thinking of might be, "What you focus on expands," which can make people feel like they're setting themselves up for a fall if they don't meet those external expectations.

When sharing your goals, it's crucial to consider how they affect your mindset. Some can serve as a motivating force; for others, they might become a source of stress. This self-fulfilling prophecy can create a cycle where the fear of failure becomes paralyzing, hindering progress. The key is to know yourself and what works best for you. If sharing your goals with an accountability partner feels more of a burden than support, focusing on internal motivation is better. Everyone has different strategies for success, and finding the right balance is essential.

Interactive Element: Finding Your Online Community

To find your ideal online community, you can start by listing your personal decluttering goals and preferences. Search for groups that align with these, using keywords like "ADHD decluttering" or "minimalist living." Join a few groups and observe their interactions. Engage with members by posting questions or sharing a small success story. Please consider how others respond and whether their experiences resonate with you. Keep exploring until you find a community that feels supportive and inspiring. This is your space to grow, learn, and connect with others who understand the unique challenges and triumphs of decluttering with ADHD.

11.2 Establishing Local Support Networks

Imagine sitting together with neighbors in a cozy living room, each person sharing stories about their cluttered spaces and the small victories they've achieved. The power of building a local support network lies in the warmth of these face-to-face interactions. Meeting in person provides a unique opportunity for encouragement and practical assistance, where gestures of support are expressed through smiles, nods, and the shared joy of overcoming challenges. These gatherings are not just about decluttering; they're about connection. The shared activities foster a sense of community, turning what could be a solitary endeavor into a collective effort. In-person interactions offer the chance to physically help each other, whether moving a piece of furniture or offering a fresh perspective on a cluttered room. The simple act of working alongside someone can transform an overwhelming task into an enjoyable, collaborative experience.

To create or join local decluttering groups, you can start by considering your existing community ties. Platforms like Meetup.com are fantastic resources for organizing meetups around shared interests, including decluttering. Consider yourself as starting a neighborhood decluttering club and inviting friends and acquaintances. You could host a book group focused on decluttering guides or minimalism, combining the joy of reading with practical applications. These groups provide a structured way to get together regularly, offering consistency and accountability. They create a space where members can share their struggles, swap decluttering tips, and celebrate successes, all while building lasting friendships.

Community decluttering events bring an added layer of camaraderie and collective action. Hosting a garage sale or swap meet can turn decluttering into a community celebration. Imagine residents of a neighborhood gathering on a sunny Saturday morning, tables set up with items they're ready to pass on. As people browse and chat, goods, stories, and encouragement are exchanged. Participating in charity drives to donate unwanted items adds a meaningful dimension, as you know your efforts are helping those in need. These events create a festive atmosphere, transforming the act of letting go into generosity and connection.

Consider the story of a small town that organized a "declutter day" in collaboration with local businesses. Shops offered discounts to participants, encouraging community members to clear out their homes and donate items to local charities. The event brought the town together, with families working side by side, chatting and laughing as they sorted their belongings. Another inspiring example comes from a community center that hosts monthly decluttering workshops. These gatherings provide a supportive environment where members learn new techniques, share firsthand experiences, and leave with renewed motivation. The workshops foster a sense of belonging and shared purpose, reinforcing that decluttering is not a solitary struggle but a communal journey.

The power of local networks lies in the genuine human connections they foster. Meeting face-to-face with others who share your goals can inspire, motivate, and provide the practical help needed to make real progress. There's something uniquely powerful about standing shoulder to shoulder with someone who understands your struggles and celebrates your successes. Whether through organized meetups, community events, or casual gatherings, these networks provide a foundation of support that can transform your decluttering efforts. Building these connections creates a nurturing environment that encourages growth, resilience, and the Happiness of less.

11.3 Sharing Success Stories and Milestones

When you recall the big and small victories in your decluttering efforts, you celebrate personal achievement and ignite a spark in others. Sharing your success story inspires your community, serving as a beacon for those who may feel stuck or overwhelmed. Each narrative is a testament to the power of perseverance, fostering a sense of pride and accomplishment. By recounting your journey, you offer hope and encouragement, showing others their goals are within reach. As you share your story, you become a catalyst for change, motivating others to embark on their paths to a clutter-free life. Your success becomes a shared triumph, building a community of individuals who believe in the possibility of transformation.

Documenting and sharing milestones effectively can amplify the impact of your story. Consider creating a visual journey through photo diaries or before-and-after galleries. These images capture the essence of transformation, providing a tangible record of progress. They are powerful motivators, illustrating what is possible with dedication and effort. Alternatively, writing blog posts or social media updates lets you share reflections and insights, connecting with a broader audience. These platforms offer a space to articulate your challenges and the strategies that worked for you. By sharing these experiences, you offer others a roadmap filled with practical lessons and encouragement. Your story becomes a valuable resource, guiding others as they navigate their decluttering challenges.

The impact of storytelling extends beyond individual motivation, strengthening community bonds, and fostering a supportive environment. Personal narratives resonate with universal challenges, creating a sense of camaraderie among those on similar journeys. By relating your experiences, you validate the struggles and triumphs of others, reinforcing the idea that they are not alone. This shared understanding fosters empathy and support, building a foundation of trust and encouragement within the community. Through storytelling, you offer inspiration and practical insights, providing others with the tools they need to succeed. Your story becomes a bridge, connecting individuals through shared experiences and collective growth.

Consider the story of Sarah, who transformed her home and lifestyle through decluttering. Her tale of perseverance and resilience inspired others in her community to act. By sharing her journey, Sarah demonstrated the power of incremental change and its profound impact on one's life. Her story motivated others to embrace minimalism, encouraging them to relinquish what no longer served them. Similarly, the account of a family who embraced minimalism and shared their journey resonated with many. Their collective effort to simplify their lives and focus on what mattered inspired others to re-evaluate their priorities. These narratives illustrate the transformative power of decluttering, offering hope and encouragement to those seeking change.

Your story, too, holds the potential to inspire and uplift others. By sharing your achievements and milestones, you contribute to a culture of support and encouragement within your community. Your experience becomes a source of strength and motivation, guiding others as they pursue their paths to a clutter-free life. In sharing your story, you become part of a collective effort to create spaces of calm and serenity where the Happiness of less is not just a concept but a lived reality. Each narrative, filled with triumphs and lessons, fosters a sense of connection and empowerment, inspiring others to believe in the possibility of transformation.

11.4 Encouragement and Accountability in Community

Imagine a gathering where laughter fills the room as people share stories of decluttering endeavors. Each tale is met with nods of understanding and words of encouragement. This is the essence of community, where encouragement and accountability play pivotal roles in sustaining motivation. Celebrating both small and significant achievements creates a powerful sense of momentum. Acknowledging even the tiniest victory, like clearing a single drawer, fuels your drive to tackle the next task. Positive reinforcement acts as a catalyst, transforming daunting challenges into manageable steps. Constructive feedback and advice, offered with kindness, guide you forward, helping you refine your strategies and approach. In this supportive environment, progress is measured by the result and the journey. You learn to appreciate the cumulative effect of small wins, each contributing to a larger sense of accomplishment.

Fostering accountability within a community involves establishing a culture of mutual responsibility and support. Regular group meetings or check-ins provide a structured framework that keeps everyone engaged and committed. These gatherings, whether held weekly or monthly, become a space for members to share updates, celebrate successes, and discuss any obstacles they may face. Setting collective goals, such as organizing a specific area of the home, unites the group with a common purpose. Tracking progress together not only reinforces accountability but also builds a sense of camaraderie. Knowing others count on you adds extra motivation to stay on the course. The shared responsibility fosters a sense of belonging, where each member feels valued and supported in their efforts.

Community-driven challenges are a dynamic way to engage and motivate members. Organizing decluttering sprints or contests injecting fun and excitement into the process. Imagine a friendly competition where participants race against the clock to clear a cluttered area. Whether small prizes or simple recognition, rewards add an incentive that makes the effort feel rewarding. Themed challenges, focusing on specific areas or items, such as "kitchen week" or "paper pile purge," bring variety and interest. These initiatives encourage creative thinking and problem-solving, inspiring members to approach decluttering from new angles. The collective energy generated by these challenges can be infectious, sparking renewed enthusiasm and commitment.

Consider the story of a group that thrived through mutual support and accountability. This community maintained consistent progress by implementing a buddy system, where members paired up to share goals and check-ins. This partnership fostered a sense of responsibility and encouragement, ensuring that no one felt alone in their efforts. Another community held a successful decluttering month with themed weeks, each focusing on a different area of the home. Members shared tips and celebrated milestones, creating a vibrant and dynamic atmosphere. These examples highlight the transformative power of encouragement and accountability, illustrating how a supportive community can propel individuals toward their decluttering goals.

Community threads weave in strength and resilience in the tapestry of your decluttering journey. Encouragement and accountability are the warp and weft, providing the structure and support needed to navigate the challenges and celebrate the victories. As you engage with your community, you discover the profound impact of shared experiences and collective growth. Each interaction, whether a word of praise or a moment of shared laughter, enriches your path and reinforces your commitment to a clutter-free life. In the next chapter, we will explore long-term strategies for maintaining a clutter-free environment, building on the foundation of community support to sustain your progress and cultivate a life of calm and serenity.

Chapter 12: Long-term Strategies for a Clutter-Free Life

Imagine a home where serenity reigns, each corner whispers peace, and space breathes freely. This vision is not a distant dream but an attainable reality, especially for those of you navigating the world with ADHD. The key lies in establishing routines that create and sustain order over time. A clutter-free life is not a one-time achievement but a lifestyle choice requiring ongoing attention and care. Much like tending to a garden, regular maintenance routines prevent the weeds of clutter from crowding out the beauty of your space. These routines are not rigid or overwhelming; they are gentle reminders to nurture the environment that encourages you.

Developing a routine for maintenance begins with setting daily and weekly cleaning schedules. These schedules are the scaffolding for your organized life, providing structure and predictability. A daily routine might include making your bed each morning or tidying up your workspace before ending your day. Weekly schedules can incorporate more thorough cleaning and decluttering sessions, dedicating a Saturday morning to sorting through mail or straightening up the living room. By integrating decluttering tasks into your regular household chores, you weave organization into the fabric of your everyday life. This integration is crucial, transforming decluttering from a separate activity into a natural part of your routine.

Incorporating maintenance into daily life doesn't have to be daunting. Small actions can make a significant impact when practiced consistently. A quick tidy-up before leaving a room prepares the space for your return and prevents clutter from accumulating. Allocating 15 minutes daily for a specific decluttering task can also be remarkably effective. This time can be spent organizing a drawer, sorting through a shelf, or clearing off a countertop. These short bursts of focused activity ensure that clutter is addressed before it becomes overwhelming. Over time, these habits become second nature, requiring little conscious effort yet yielding substantial benefits.

Flexibility is another vital component of maintaining a clutter-free lifestyle. Life is dynamic, and circumstances change, demanding adaptability in your routines. Adjusting your routines to accommodate new demands may be necessary during busy periods or holidays. Allowing occasional breaks is also essential to prevent burnout. Decluttering should not feel like a chore but a practice that enhances your well-being. Taking breaks ensures you return to your routines with renewed energy and motivation.

Consider the story of a parent who involves their children in daily tidying tasks. Each evening, as part of their bedtime routine, they spend a few minutes together picking up toys and cleaning the living room. This practice maintains order and teaches valuable skills to the children, fostering a sense of responsibility and teamwork. Another example is a professional who uses their commute time to plan decluttering goals. By reflecting on what needs attention during their drive home, they arrive ready to tackle specific tasks, making the most of their limited time.

12.2 Interactive Element: Create Your Routine

Take a moment to outline your ideal maintenance routine. Start by listing daily and weekly tasks that would support a clutter-free environment. Consider the natural rhythms of your day and week and identify where these tasks can fit seamlessly. Remember to include moments for rest and flexibility, ensuring your routine is sustainable and enjoyable.

Creating and maintaining a clutter-free life is a continuous process that adapts with you over time. As you establish these routines, they become the foundation of your organized space, supporting the calm and serenity you seek. Each day presents an opportunity to nurture your environment, making room for peace and clarity.

12.3 Celebrating Success and Reflecting on Progress

You must celebrate every gram of success you achieve. Picture this: you have just cleared out a cluttered room, and the space now feels open, inviting, and full of potential. This is not just about tidying up a room; it's a milestone in your decluttering efforts. Celebrating these achievements is crucial, boosting morale and reinforcing your hard work. Imagine hosting a small gathering to display your new, organized space. Invite friends and family, share your journey, and admire your efforts. This validates your accomplishment and inspires others. Or consider treating yourself to a well-deserved reward after reaching a primary decluttering goal—a favorite meal, a day out, or perhaps a new plant for your rejuvenated space. Each celebration is a moment to savor your success, encouraging and motivating you to keep moving forward.

Tracking and reflecting on your progress is equally important. It provides insight into the practical methods and areas that might need adjustment. Keeping a journal to document your thoughts and feelings about the process can be incredibly revealing. Write about your struggles, breakthroughs, and moments of clarity; each entry offers a more in-depth understanding of your relationship with your environment. Creating a visual timeline or collage of before-and-after photos is another powerful tool. By visually mapping your progress, you see the tangible results of your hard work, which can be immensely gratifying and motivating. These tools help you track your achievements and allow you to reflect on the emotional journey of decluttering.

Reflection is more than a retrospective glance; it catalyzes ongoing success. Regular self-assessment helps maintain momentum and fosters continuous improvement. Analyzing the best strategies gives you valuable insights for planning future actions and objectives.

Decluttering style. You may have already discovered that tackling one small area at a time prevents overwhelm or that involving a friend can make the process more enjoyable. You can use these insights to set new goals, refining your approach based on past achievements. This iterative process ensures your efforts align with your evolving needs and lifestyle, keeping you motivated and focused. Consider the story of a retiree who writes monthly reflections on their minimalist journey. They use this time to reassess their possessions, ensuring their living space reflects their current values and priorities. These reflections have helped them maintain a clutter-free home and deepened their appreciation for the simplicity and freedom that minimalism brings. Similarly, a student reviews their progress at the end of each semester. This practice allows them to declutter their study space, evaluate their organizational habits, and set goals for the upcoming term. Acknowledging their progress and adapting their strategies, they maintain an environment conducive to learning and personal growth.

Reflection Section: Journal Prompt

Please take a moment to reflect on your decluttering journey so far. What have been your most significant challenges and successes? How has your relationship with space evolved? Write about these experiences in a journal, noting emerging patterns or insights.

Consider setting one new goal and outlining a plan based on your reflections.

In the grand tapestry of life, decluttering is more than merely sorting and discarding. It is a practice of transformation, where celebrating victories and reflecting on progress weave together the threads of a life lived with intention and clarity.

Ongoing Adaptation to Life Changes

Life is a series of transitions, bringing its own set of challenges and opportunities. For those of you with ADHD, these shifts might feel daunting, but they also present a chance to reassess and refine your approach to decluttering. Flexibility and openness to change are your greatest allies in maintaining a clutter-free lifestyle. Imagine moving to a new home or downsizing; these are perfect moments to let go of items that no longer serve you. Each box packed is an opportunity to decide if its contents genuinely fit into the next chapter of your life. Similarly, changes in family dynamics, like welcoming a new baby or adjusting to an empty nest, call for a fresh look at the spaces and stuff that define your home. These life shifts are invitations to tailor your environment to your current needs, ensuring it supports your well-being and daily activities.

Re-evaluating your possessions and routines regularly is crucial. Inventory checks can help identify what is necessary and what can be released. It's like taking a snapshot of your life, assessing which items are part of your story. This doesn't have to be a cumbersome task, it's a seasonal activity, much like spring cleaning. As you sift through your belongings, consider their function and relevance to your present lifestyle. Reorganizing spaces to accommodate new functions or priorities brings new life into your home. For instance, a spare room might transform into a home office, a craft space, or a serene retreat. Such adjustments ensure that your environment evolves alongside your life, reflecting who you are and where you're headed.

Continuous learning and growth should be at the heart of your decluttering journey. Seek innovative ideas and approaches to keep the process fresh and engaging. Attend workshops or read books on organization and minimalism to discover different perspectives and techniques. These resources can spark inspiration, offering innovative solutions to familiar challenges. Joining online forums can also be incredibly rewarding. They provide a platform to exchange tips and experiences with others on a similar path, fostering a sense of community and support. This collective wisdom can guide you through transitions, offering insights you might not have considered.

Please look at the story of a couple who downsized after retirement. They embraced the opportunity to simplify their lives, focusing on quality over quantity. Each belonging was carefully considered, leading to a streamlined, peaceful home that matched their new pace of life. Their story exemplifies how adapting to intentional changes can bring profound satisfaction and freedom. Also, could you think about a young professional who adapted their space for remote work? They transformed a cluttered spare room into a functional office with organized storage and a calming aesthetic. This adaptation improved their productivity and created a sanctuary for focus and creativity.

These narratives illustrate the power of adaptability in maintaining a clutter-free lifestyle. By viewing life's changes as opportunities for growth, you can approach decluttering with renewed energy and purpose. Embrace the ebb and flow of life, allowing your environment to shift and change alongside you. Each transition is a chance to refine your space, ensuring it serves your evolving needs and aspirations. As you navigate these changes, remember that your home reflects you—a dynamic living space supporting your journey toward an organized, serene life.

12.5 Embracing the Journey: A Lifetime of Clarity

As you step into decluttering, viewing this endeavor not as a one-time task but as a continuous process of refining your environment and, consequently, yourself is essential. It's about adopting a lifelong learning and growth mindset, understanding that clarity is a journey, not a destination. Each day offers a chance to explore new ways of simplifying life, embracing the slight changes that lead to greater clarity. Finding joy in this ongoing process is essential. Each item you choose to keep or let go of is part of a narrative that defines your space and, by extension, your state of mind. Revel in the satisfaction of knowing that you are shaping your surroundings to support your aspirations and well-being better.

Living with clarity and intention has profound benefits beyond a tidy home. Maintaining a clutter-free lifestyle enhances your mental well-being, reducing the stress and anxiety that clutter often brings. When your physical environment is organized, your mind can relax, allowing you to focus on what truly matters. This sense of order brings greater freedom and flexibility in daily life. Without the constant distraction of clutter, you can pursue your passions and explore new experiences. Imagine the relief of knowing exactly where everything is, the time saved by not searching for lost items, and the mental space freed up to think creatively and make better decisions. Clarity is the foundation of a balanced and fulfilling life.

To inspire you on this path, consider the stories of individuals who have embraced simplicity and found profound fulfillment. Take the digital nomad who chose to prioritize experiences over possessions. Shedding unnecessary belongings, they created a life rich in adventures and meaningful connections. Their focus shifted from accumulating things to gathering moments, creating a sense of freedom and Happiness. Or think of the family who adopted a minimalist lifestyle to strengthen their relationships. By reducing material distractions, they fostered more profound bonds, finding joy in shared experiences rather than in things. These narratives highlight the transformative power of living with clarity, illustrating how letting go can open doors to new possibilities.

In the words of thought leaders in minimalism and mindfulness, "The things you own end up owning you." This quote serves as a powerful reminder of the weight possessions can carry. It encourages you to evaluate what truly enriches your life and to let go of anything that doesn't serve your highest good. Another insight comes from mindfulness: "Simplicity is the ultimate sophistication." This speaks to the elegance of a pared-down existence, where the beauty of life shines when distractions are removed. These words inspire a shift in perspective, urging you to embrace the simplicity that comes with clarity and intention.

Embracing a clutter-free life is not about deprivation but making room for what truly matters. It's about creating a space that reflects your values and supports your dreams. Choosing clarity invites peace and serenity into your home and your heart. Imagine the possibilities that unfold when you are no longer weighed down by excess. Picture a life where every decision aligns with your true desires and your environment nurtures your growth and creativity.

This is the essence of living with clarity—a lifetime of discovery and fulfillment, where the Happiness of less becomes a guiding principle. As you continue this path, remember that each step is a celebration of progress, a testament to your commitment to a life of clarity and purpose.

Conclusion

As we close this journey together, let's take a moment to reflect on the path we've traveled. We've explored the intricate connection between ADHD and clutter and discovered how the whirlwind of clutter can mirror the internal chaos many of us feel. Yet, we have also seen how you can transform that chaos into clarity with short, focused bursts of effort. By dedicating just 15 minutes daily, you can see tangible changes in your environment and, more importantly, in your mind.

This book is a testament to the power of mindfulness and minimalism. By embracing these concepts, you can unlock a life filled with peace and order. Decluttering is more than just tidying up; it's about creating an environment that supports your goals and aspirations. It's about finding the Happiness of less and allowing space for what truly matters.

From the beginning, the emphasis has been on setting realistic goals. Breaking down tasks into manageable steps can prevent overwhelming and foster a sense of achievement. Leveraging tools and apps can streamline this process, making tracking your progress and staying motivated easier. Mindful reflection has been another cornerstone of our approach. It allows you to address the emotional attachments that often hold you back, helping you let go with gratitude. The benefits of decluttering are profound. Imagine a home where every item has its place, where your surroundings reflect your inner calm. Improved focus, reduced stress, and enhanced organizational skills are just a few of the outcomes you can expect. These changes create a more serene living environment, paving the way for true Happiness and clarity.

To remind you, decluttering is not a one-time event. It's a lifelong journey. As your life evolves, so will your needs and priorities. Regularly reassess your spaces and routines to ensure they align with your current goals. Flexibility is key; adapt as you grow, and let your environment grow.

I would like you to act as soon as possible. Choose a small area in your home and dedicate 15 minutes to it this week. Start small and build momentum, whether it's a drawer, a shelf, or a corner of your room. You'll be amazed at the impact of these short, focused sessions.

As you embark on this journey, remember that community plays a vital role. Connect with others on similar paths, share your progress, and offer support. Whether online or in person, these connections foster encouragement and accountability. Together, you can inspire and uplift one another, reinforcing the belief that change is possible. Looking ahead, envision the freedom, clarity, and fulfillment that await you with a clutter-free lifestyle. Picture a serene home that feels like a sanctuary place where you can thrive, free from the distractions of unnecessary possessions. You can create this life filled with intention, simplicity, and joy.

Thank you for allowing me to be part of your journey. My experiences with clutter and ADHD have shaped my belief in the transformative power of decluttering. I am confident in your ability to achieve lasting change. You have the tools, the support, and the determination needed to succeed.

As you move forward, hold onto this powerful truth: the Happiness of less is within your reach. Embrace the calmness that comes with a straightforward, organized life. You have already taken the first step, and each subsequent step will bring you closer to the life you envision. Remember, you are not alone on this path. Together, we can create a world where clutter no longer holds you back, where clarity and peace are possible in every area of your life.

Review

Your feedback on this book would be greatly appreciated. It is my sincere hope that it assists you in embarking on the journey towards minimalism and a more fulfilling life. May this book provide you with the tranquility, clarity, and organization you seek. Additionally, I encourage you to read the chapters on the role of humor in decluttering and essential cleaning tips, as cleanliness is an integral part of the process.

Thank you for reading my book.

Tess.R

Amazon Review
https://www/amazon.com/re
view/review-
create/9798312176513

 for the hardback

Or   as   above   with
97983085614 for the softback
cover.

Or Just Scan the easy-peasy
lemon-squeezy QR Code, and
Hey, Presto! You will be on the
Amazon Review page!

Chapter 13

FAQ: the frequently asked questions. Followed by Reasons to Declutter, it's a look at some funny and bizarre things—YES, a look at some things that might make you laugh aloud!

I have done this before, but it never worked. Why would now?

It's understandable to feel disheartened if past attempts have not worked out. The journey to declutter, especially with ADHD, can be challenging and require patience and persistence. But here is why it might be different this time:

New Strategies: Sometimes, it's about finding the right approach. The strategies are explicitly tailored for ADHD so they could make a significant difference.

Small Wins Matter: Instead of trying to tackle everything at once, focus on smaller, more manageable tasks. Celebrate those small victories to stay motivated.

Support Systems: Having a support system, whether it's friends, family, or even online communities, can provide encouragement and accountability.

Understanding Yourself: Each attempt teaches you more about what works for you and what does not. Use that insight to refine your approach.

Flexibility: Be flexible and kind to yourself. If a specific method does not work, it is okay to try a different one.

It is not about perfection; it is about progress. You have got this!

Tackling decluttering with ADHD is no small feat. However, there are a few reasons why this time might be different:

Tailored Strategies: This time, you are armed with approaches designed explicitly for ADHD. It is not just about decluttering but finding methods that work uniquely for you.

Incremental Progress: Focusing on small, manageable tasks can help you see progress without feeling overwhelmed. This is not about a massive overhaul in one day. It is about steady, consistent steps.

Mindset Shift: Recognizing past attempts as learning experiences rather than failures can be empowering. Each attempt teaches you something valuable about what works and what does not.

Support: Whether from books, support groups, or friends, having friends on your side can make the journey less daunting.

Flexibility and Patience: Giving yourself the grace to try different approaches and not being too hard on yourself if things do not go perfectly can make a significant difference.

Remember, it is not about being perfect. It's about making progress. Each small step forward is a victory. You have the tools and the potential to make it work this time.

Why will this be any different? Can you guarantee it will **work?**

I can understand feeling doubtful after past experiences, and while I can't guarantee success, I believe that with the right approach, there's potential for a different outcome. Here is why:

Personalized Approach: You seek strategies explicitly tailored for ADHD, which means these methods are designed with your unique needs in mind.

Incremental Wins: Focusing on small, achievable tasks can build momentum and confidence. It is about progress, not perfection.

Learning from Past Attempts: Each previous try has given new insights into what did not work. Use that knowledge to refine your approach.

Support and Resources: A solid support system and resource access can make a significant difference.

Mindset Shift: Viewing this as a journey rather than a one-time fix can help manage expectations and reduce frustration.

While there are no guarantees in life, every small step you take toward decluttering creates a more organized and manageable space. Your persistence and willingness to try again are strengths.

I do not want to get rid of everything I love.

Decluttering is not about losing everything you hold dear. It's about creating space for the things that truly matter to you, relieving the overwhelming burden of clutter, and fostering a sense of hope and optimism.

Here are some strategies to help you keep what you love while decluttering:

Sentimental Items: Choose a special box or space to store sentimental items. This way, they are not mixed with everyday clutter, and you know exactly where to find them.

Create Boundaries: Limit the number of certain types of items you can keep. For example, if you love books, choose a specific number of shelves or space to house them.

Keep the things that bring you joy and serve a purpose. This will help you decide what stays and what goes, keeping you connected to the inspiration behind each item.

Rotation System: If you have items you love but do not use often, consider a rotation system where you swap them in and out of use. This keeps things fresh without adding clutter.

Digitize: Consider digitizing items like photos or documents. This way, you can keep the memories without the physical space they occupy.

One In, One Out: Implement a rule that something old must go for every latest item you bring into your home. This will help maintain balance.

Ask for Help: Sometimes, having a friend or family member's assistance can provide a distinct perspective and make the process less daunting.

Remember, the goal is to create a space that supports your well-being and reduces stress, not to strip away the things you love. It is all about balance and finding what works best for you.

I do not want to do these mammoth tasks; my house is a mess in every room.

I get it. Tackling the whole house can feel overwhelming. The key is to break it down into smaller, manageable tasks and take it step by step. Here are some strategies that might help:

Start Small: To begin with, pick one small area. It could be a single drawer, a shelf, or a corner of a room.

Set a Timer: Give yourself a set amount of time, like 15 or 30 minutes, to work on decluttering. When the timer goes off, you can stop for the day or take a break.

Do Daily Tasks: Instead of trying to do everything at once, set small daily goals. For example, tackle one drawer today and one shelf tomorrow.

Use the Four-Box Method: Get four boxes and label them: **Keep, Donate/Recycle, Trash, Relocate.** Please place your items in the appropriate box as you go through them.

Reward Yourself: After completing a small task, it's essential to reward yourself with something you enjoy.

This can be a favorite snack, a relaxing activity, or downtime.

Get Help: If possible, enlist the help of friends or family. Sometimes, having someone there makes the process less daunting and more manageable.

Remember, it's about progress, not perfection. Celebrate the small wins, and don't worry about perfecting everything. What matters is that you're moving forward, which should encourage and motivate you.

It is all about taking one step at a time and gradually progressing.

Pick a Starting Point: Start with a small area, such as your desk, a drawer, or a corner of a room.

Gather Supplies: Get four boxes or bins and label them: Keep, Donate, Trash, and Relocate.

Set a Timer: Give yourself 15-30 minutes. This keeps the task manageable and reduces overwhelm.

Sort Items: Start sorting items in your chosen area into the four boxes. Be decisive but kind to yourself.

Take a Break: Take a short break once the timer goes off. Celebrate the small win!

Rinse and Repeat: If you feel up to it, repeat the process in another small area. If not, that is okay— Tomorrow is another day.

I do not give a flying Fick, so what? I will give it only one more chance!

That is the spirit! Sometimes, a bit of defiance is just what we need to get things moving. Let us start small and see where it takes us.

Pick a tiny area—a single drawer or a room corner. Set a timer for 15 minutes and focus on that one spot. Remember, it's about progress, not perfection. You've got this, and I'm here to cheer you on every step of the way.

I am exasperated with all this. If you do it this way or that way, it will ultimately return to the same old chaos.

I understand it is frustrating to feel stuck in an endless cycle. But recognizing this pattern is a decisive first step toward breaking it. Here is a different approach that might help:

1. Acceptance and Incremental Change

2. Accept Chaos: Sometimes, the first step is accepting that some level of chaos may always be present. Embrace it as part of your environment.

3. Small Wins Matter: Focus on small, manageable changes. Even spending just 5 minutes each day on a tiny area can add up over time.

It is habits over perfection. Develop simple, easy-to-maintain habits. For example, commit to putting away five items every evening before bed.

Functional Over Ideal: Aim for a functional space rather than a perfectly organized one. Think about what will make your daily life easier and more efficient.

Regular Resets: To maintain order, schedule regular, short "reset" sessions, which could be weekly or biweekly.

Self-Compassion: Be kind to yourself. Understand that progress, not perfection, is the goal. Acknowledge each small achievement.

Support Systems: Accountability Partners: Find someone to check in with regularly to enable a support system to monitor and support your progress in the background.

Consider Professional Help:
Consider hiring a professional organizer who understands ADHD. They can provide personalized strategies and support to help you manage your clutter and create a space that works for you.

This is not about changing everything overnight. It's about finding sustainable ways to make small, meaningful changes that gradually improve your space and peace of mind. You have this!

Take a deep breath and try to give yourself some grace. It's okay to feel exasperated, and it is also OK to ask for help when you need it. I am here to support you every step of the way.

Take it one step at a time. What is one tiny thing you could manage today? Could you pick up a few items or organize a small space like a bedside table?

How can I make it work this time?

Feeling apprehensive about trying again is natural, but it could be different with new strategies and a fresh perspective this time. Here is a step-by-step plan to help you make it work:

1. Start Small and Celebrate Wins

2. Choose One Small Area: Pick a small, manageable area, like a single drawer or a part of a shelf.

3. Set a Timer: Work for a set amount of time, like 15-20 minutes. This helps keep the task from feeling overwhelming.

Celebrate Your Progress: Acknowledge and celebrate even the most minor victories. Each step forward is progress.

1. Develop Simple yet Sustainable Habits

2. Daily Quick Tidy: Spend 5-10 minutes at the end of each day putting things back in their place.

The One-in-One-out Rule is to remove one old item for every new item you bring into your home. It is the same as OHIO: Only handle it once!

Create Drop Zones: Designate specific spots for keys, mail, and daily essentials to prevent clutter from building up.

Visualize the Benefits, the lovely, tidy, decluttered areas!

Picture the Outcome: Visualize how a decluttered space will improve your daily life: less stress, more focus, and a feeling of accomplishment.

Ask for Help

Accountability Partner: Find a friend or family member with whom you can check in regularly. This can provide motivation and support.

Be Kind to Yourself

Progress, Not Perfection: Focus on making progress rather than achieving perfection. It is okay to have setbacks.

Celebrate Small Wins: Every small step is toward a more organized space.

Focus on making progress rather than achieving perfection. Each small step forward is a victory, and setbacks are part of the journey.

Acknowledge and celebrate every small achievement. Each step forward, no matter how small, is a step toward a more organized space!

Use Baskets and Bins:

Organize related items together in baskets or bins. This can make it easier to find things and keep your space tidy.

Label Everything:

Labeling drawers, bins, and shelves can help you and others in your household know where things belong, making it easier to maintain order.

Digitize Paper Clutter:

Reduce paper clutter by digitizing essential documents. Scan them and store them in cloud storage for easy access and organization.

Create Routines and Habits.

Establishing simple routines can help you maintain organization. For example, set aside weekly time to declutter a specific area or handle paperwork.

You can gradually create a more organized and functional space by breaking down the process into manageable steps and incorporating sustainable habits. Remember, it is a journey, and each step you take is toward a calmer, more organized life.

Procrastination Phrases: Acronyms!

W.A.I.T.: Why Am I Tired?

Use this to discuss how procrastination can often stem from underlying exhaustion and how recognizing this can lead to more effective time management.

C.R.A.S.H.: Cannot Really Accept Starting Here

Explore the mental barriers that prevent starting tasks and strategies to overcome these initial hurdles.

L.O.S.T.: Lack of Simple Tidying

Discuss how simple daily habits can prevent clutter from accumulating and how ADHD makes this particularly challenging.

H.O.L.D.: Hoping Organization Lingers Daily

Delve into the hope that the organization will somehow maintain itself and provide practical tips to make it a reality.

P.A.U.S.E.: Procrastinating and Undermining Simple Efforts

Talk about how small acts of procrastination can undermine overall efforts and how to stay motivated.

S.T.A.L.L.: Still Trying and Letting Linger

Address the issue of letting tasks linger and strategies to keep momentum.

R.E.S.I.S.T.: Reluctant Every Second I Start Tidying

Highlight the reluctance to start and how to find motivation to get going.

A.V.O.I.D.: Abandoning Various Obligations in Decluttering

Discuss how avoiding tasks contributes to clutter and how to tackle obligations head-on.

W.A.N.D.E.R.: Worrying About Not Doing Efficiently Right

Explore perfectionism that can lead to procrastination and how to accept "good enough."

D.R.A.G.: Don't Really Attempt Getting Organized.

Please discuss the feeling of dragging one's feet and tips to jumpstart the process.

D.E.L.A.Y.: Deciding Everything Later and Yawn

Address how indecision leads to delays and ways to make quicker decisions.

P.U.T.: Procrastinate Until Tomorrow

Discuss the habit of putting things off and how to break the cycle.

B.R.A.K.E.: Being Reluctant About Keeping Everything

Highlight the reluctance to part with items and strategies for decluttering with purpose.

N.E.S.T.: Never Ending Stuff Troubles

Explore the ongoing battle with clutter and how to manage it sustainably.

C.L.U.T.T.E.R.: Constantly Leaving Untouched Things Everywhere Randomly

Discuss the tendency to leave items everywhere and tips for creating organized spaces.

S.L.O.W.: Simply Leaving Objects Wherever

Address the habit of dropping items and how to cultivate mindfulness in tidying up.

M.E.S.S.: Might Eventually Start Sorting

Explore procrastination in sorting and give tips to make the process more appealing.

H.A.L.T.: Hardly Attempting to Let Go of Things

Discuss the emotional attachment to items and how to let go.

J.A.M.: Justifying All Mess: Highlight our justifications for clutter and how to challenge these beliefs.

Q.U.I.T.: Questioning Unnecessary Items Temporarily

Explore the process of questioning items' necessity and how to make decisions.

Entertaining reasons why I should not do this...

I should not bother to put it into my trolley or basket or whatever, so let us dive into some lighthearted reasons why you might want to keep your hands off the decluttering cart:

A Chaotic Home Is a Treasure Hunt: Why look for excitement elsewhere when every trip to the kitchen can become an adventure? You never know what you might find in that pile—your keys, yesterday's snacks, or long-lost treasures!

Embrace the Creative Mess: After all, the mess is just evidence of creativity in action. Who needs a sterile, perfectly organized space where you can be the proud owner of a "creativity explosion"?

Decluttering is for the Faint-Hearted: Real warriors live in organized chaos. It signifies resilience and the ability to thrive in challenging environments. Who needs to follow the crowd when you can boldly stand out?

Clutter Keeps You Fit: Have you ever considered the physical benefits of clutter? Navigating through your stuff is an obstacle course. It's like having a free gym at home!

It is a Personality Statement: Why conform to boring societal norms of neatness? Let your clutter reflect your life's vibrant, dynamic, and unpredictable nature. Your home is just an extension of your unique self.

Conversation Starter: Your house becomes a talking point for guests. They will never have a dull moment trying to guess what is hidden under that pile of magazines or why a yoga mat is in the bathroom.

Clutter is an Insurance Policy: Have you ever lost something valuable? With enough clutter, it is bound to show up... eventually. Think of it as nature's way of keeping things safe, albeit slightly chaotic.

Future Archaeology Site: Imagine the joy of future generations discovering layers of your life. Each stratum of mess tells a story. You are creating a time capsule!

Suspense and Mystery: Every day is like living in a suspense novel. Did you put the TV remote in the fridge again? Only time will tell...

Last-Minute Cleaning Marathon: Why spread out cleaning over time when you can get a thrilling, high-adrenaline rush by doing it all in a marathon session right before guests arrive?

Seasonal Surprises: Decorating for the holidays is way more fun when you must dig through your belongings to find your decorations. Every season becomes a surprise party!

Healthy Procrastination: Delaying tasks builds character. Plus, it gives you ample time to think deeply about the most optimal way to arrange those socks... someday.

OTHER AMUSING THINGS TO PONDER....

Book Titles on Decluttering

"Why Is There a Toaster in My Closet? Tackling Clutter, One Surprise at a Time"

"Who Put the Milk Carton in the Microwave? Finding Calm in Clutter Chaos"

It is a playful take that captures the ADHD habit of placing items in unexpected locations.

"Why Can't I Find Anything?!: Organizing for the Perpetually Distracted."

"Help, There's a Sock in My Fridge! A Fun Approach to ADHD Decluttering"

Exaggerates the humor of misplaced items to make the decluttering process less intimidating.

Funny Yet Practical Book Titles:

"Oops, Where Did I Put That? Decluttering for Distracted Minds"

This is a humorous reflection of the ADHD struggle with forgetfulness.

"This Isn't Where That Goes! A Survival Guide for ADHD Clutter"

Lightheartedly addresses the issue of misplaced or "homeless" items.

Book titles, including Decluttering.

"How Did My Keys End Up in the Freezer? ADHD Decluttering Made Simple"

Combines humor with practical advice to appeal to overwhelmed readers.

"Why Is There a Ladder in My Bathroom? A Fun Guide to Decluttering Chaos"

A book title that encourages laughter at the absurdity of clutter without judgment.

"Wait, Wasn't This Clean Yesterday? ADHD Decluttering for Real Life"

Speaks to the frustration of recurring messes in a humorous and understanding tone.

Over-the-Top ADHD Humor Titles:

"Why Do I Have 27 Coffee Mugs? Conquering ADHD Clutter Without Guilt"

Lightheartedly pokes fun at the tendency to accumulate duplicates while being supportive.

"There's a Pizza Box Under My Bed: A No-Shame Guide to Decluttering"

It is a dramatic yet relatable example that embraces the mess with humor.

"Wait, What's in This Drawer Again? Decluttering for ADHD Minds"

Acknowledges the ADHD habit of creating "mystery" drawers or hiding spots for your stash of goodies!

"How Did I End Up with 15 Sets of Scissors? ADHD Decluttering Made Fun"

A playful jab at the accumulation of duplicates, with an upbeat approach to organizing.

Empowering and Transformative Book Titles

"Tame the Chaos: Decluttering for the Overwhelmed Mind"

Highlights regaining control over clutter in a relatable, uplifting way.

"Organized, Not Overwhelmed: A Guide to Clearing Your Space and Mind"

Directly appeals to adults with ADHD by addressing both physical and mental clutter.

"The Clarity Cure: Breaking Free from Clutter's Grip"

Humorous and Relatable

"Help, I Lost My Keys in the Fridge: Decluttering for ADHD Minds"

It is a quirky, relatable title that grabs attention and makes readers feel seen.

"Oops, I Bought That Twice: The ADHD Guide to Simplifying Your Stuff so you don't buy duplicate items."

Playfully acknowledges common ADHD challenges while offering solutions.

"Why Is There a Toaster in My Closet? Taming the ADHD Clutter Monster"

"Clear the Chaos: Simple Steps to a Manageable Home"

It focuses on breaking clutter into manageable steps, perfect for ADHD readers.

"Less Stuff, Less Stress: A Decluttering Guide for Distracted Minds"

Highlights how decluttering can reduce stress and overwhelm.

"From Overwhelmed to Organized: How to Simplify Any Space"

Metaphorical and Intriguing

"The ADHD Reset: Declutter Your Space, Declutter Your Mind"

Suggests a holistic transformation, tying physical clutter to mental clarity.

"The Untangling: How to Free Yourself from Life's Messes"

"Breaking the Clutter Cycle: A New Path to Peaceful Living"

Addresses the repetitive nature of clutter, offering a path to lasting change.

On Overwhelm

1. "The first step in decluttering is to breathe deeply. The second step is to put down the wine glass— decluttering tipsy is just shopping in reverse."

2. "Don't look at the whole house as a project. Start small. Like, small. That junk drawer? It's your Mount Everest today."

3. "Overwhelmed? Just tackle one thing. Start with that sock that hasn't had a partner since 2018."

4. Your brain says, 'I might need this someday.' Reality says, "You haven't needed it in five years.' Logic says, 'Toss it.' Your heart says, 'But it's shiny!"

5."If guilt were an Olympic sport, decluttering would be the triathlon."

6. "I get it—you keep the ugly vase because your mother-in-law gave it to you. Here's a thought: keep the memory, lose the vase. Your shelves will thank you."

Other Decluttering stuff!

1. "ADHD decluttering feels a bit like herding cats—if the cats were also on roller skates and highly sentimental about their skate collection and readily got very tearful about the smallest things!

2. "You do not own clutter; clutter owns you. And it has been charging you rent in stress for years.

3. "ADHD brains love chaos until it turns into 'Where are my keys?' followed by 'Who stole my keys?!' before realizing they're in the fridge." After accusations were made regarding the partner...oops!

4. "This is not clutter; it is a memory museum. Admission? My sanity."

5. "I'd declutter today, but I'm pretty sure the dust bunnies unionized."

6. "No, that box in the corner is not junk—it is my 'someday project.' Someday has not RSVP'd yet."

7. "A label maker won't fix your clutter, but it will make it look professional."

8. "You don't need a new shelf for your stuff—you need fewer reasons to buy another lamp." How many does one need?

On Decluttering as Self-Care
"Think of decluttering as therapy for your space. The bonus? No co-pay."

"A clutter-free room is like a spa day for your brain—minus the face pack and the overpriced robes."

MYTHS, TALES & THINGS AROUND DECLUTTERING!

Myth 1. You must get Rid of Everything!
Reality: "This isn't Survivor: Home Edition—you don't have to vote your belongings off the island. It's about creating harmony, not a house so empty you hear echoes."

Myth 2: "Organized People Are Born That Way."
Reality: "No one emerges from the womb clutching a color-coded planner. If they did, their parents would probably lose it in the diaper bag."

Myth 3: "If It's Not Perfect, It's Not Worth Doing."
Reality: "Perfection is overrated. You win if you can find your keys or the remotes without a scavenger hunt."

Myth 4: "Decluttering Is a One-and-Done Job."
Reality: "Decluttering is like laundry: no matter how much you do, there's always another load waiting. The trick is to stay ahead of the sock pile."

Myth 5: "You Have to Be Ruthless."
Reality: "This isn't a reality TV competition. You don't have to eliminate 80% of your wardrobe to win a cash prize—though you might discover you've been hoarding a decade's worth of unmatched socks."

Myth 6: "Decluttering Takes Forever"
Reality: "Forever is a long time. Decluttering is like a Netflix binge—you can knock out a good chunk in an afternoon, especially if snacks are involved."

Myth 7: "Only Marie Kondo Can Help You."

Reality: "Marie Kondo is great, but so is your intuition. You don't need to thank your T-shirts before donating them. A polite nod will do."

Discover why traditional organizing methods fail and how to create a system that works for you.

Learn the one mindset shift that makes decluttering achievable—even with ADHD.

Overcome decision fatigue with proven techniques for making fast, stress-free choices.

Break free from guilt and learn to let go of items without regret.

Create an ADHD-friendly "clutter circuit" to streamline tidying and avoid overwhelming.

You should be able to answer these questions if you have read this book!

Find out how to organize sentimental items without feeling emotionally drained.

Learn why "perfect organization" is a myth and how to embrace progress instead.

Unlock the secret to creating routines that work even on chaotic days.

Gain actionable tips for tackling cluttered areas in short, manageable bursts.

Stop the cycle of re-cluttering with strategies to make the organization stick.

Discover why your brain thrives in visual environments—and how to use that to your advantage.

Master the art of "priority decluttering" for immediate wins in your space.

Learn how to set realistic goals that align with your energy and focus.

Get step-by-step guidance for organizing standard clutter zones like desks, closets, and pantries.

Discover how to make decluttering fun and rewarding instead of frustrating.

Conquer the emotional attachment to clutter with practical strategies.

Transform your space without giving up the items that bring you joy.

Learn ADHD-specific tips for staying on track during a decluttering session. Avoid the traps of perfectionism and learn why "good enough" and not perfection is the secret to success.

Discover how many of the earlier statements can be fixed by decluttering. A clutter-free space can also improve focus, reduce stress, and boost mood—all this again through decluttering! After reading my book, I hope you have discovered most, if not all, of the answers to the previous statements. If not,

Re-read my book, please!

Add some Over-the-Top Decluttering Analogies

Turn mundane tasks into epic battles.

"Clearing the freezer wasn't just decluttering—it was an archaeological dig into the Ice Age. I half-expected to find a mammoth steak labeled '2013.'"

Dramatize Decision Paralysis

Bring attention to how ridiculous decision-making can feel:

"Should I keep this chipped mug? It's not just a mug— it's a symbol of my college days, my love for coffee, and my complete inability to let go of ceramic sentimentality."

Create a "Mythical Guide" Section

Introduce a quirky fictional helper.

"Meet Sir Toss-A-Lot, the fearless knight whose sole purpose is to vanquish clutter dragons. His motto? 'When in doubt, throw it out!' He's a bit dramatic, but he gets the job done."

Riff on Decluttering Trends

Gently poke fun at popular methods.

"Does this cheese grater spark joy? No, but it sparked some serious knuckle injuries last Thanksgiving. Into the discard pile, you go!

Decluttering Humor One-Liners!

"I cleaned out my junk drawer... and discovered I might be a pirate. How else do you explain three compasses and no treasure?"

"Decluttering feels like solving a mystery. Who bought this? Why? And the biggest question—why do I still have it?"

"Minimalists say less is more.' My attic says, 'Let's not get carried away."

"I didn't lose weight this year, but my closet did—it dropped 20 pounds of clothes I swore I'd fit into again."

"Decluttering Rule #1: You'll need it as soon as you throw something out. Decluttering Rule #2: You'll forget you threw it out and blame your partner."

Funny Decluttering Scenarios!

1. The Great 'Just in Case' Debate:

"Do I need this 10-year-old phone charger? No. But what if one day, it's 2040, and I stumble across a Nokia that can save the world?"

2. The Sentimental Chaos Collector: You try to declutter a drawer.

You find a broken pen.

Reflective thoughts: "This pen was used to compose a love letter to my first significant partner, and I also discovered avocados at a discounted price. Can I let it go?"

Decluttering with ADHD: You start cleaning out the drawer further. You find: A birthday card from 2005.

A receipt for "mystery cheese."

Half a deck of Uno cards.

Then—suddenly—you are halfway through re-reading all your old yearbooks, the drawer's still open, and it is three hours later.

Overheard During Decluttering:

"If I throw away the instruction manual, it's guaranteed to break tomorrow."

"These socks don't match, but they've been through a lot together."

"This box of tangled cords is Schrödinger's tech graveyard— it's

everything and nothing at once"

Part Two: Unique and Inspirational Decluttering Tales

Here are two short, human-centered tales with surprising & touching twists:

Story 1: The Shoebox of Secrets
Sometimes clutter is more than it seems.

Sara had a shoebox under her bed. For years, it moved with her from house to house. She never opened it, but she could not part with it. One decluttering day, she finally lifted the lid. Inside were birthday cards her late grandmother had written—one for every birthday of Sara's life. Her grandmother had passed before giving her the last ones.

Sara cried. She read every card. Then, she selected just three to keep and framed them. The rest? She let go— because she realized the real treasure was not the cards. It was the memory of her grandmother's love that had been with her all along.

Lesson: Sometimes, decluttering is not about loss but finding what matters.

Story 2: The Sweater and the Stranger
Bella was downsizing her wardrobe. At the bottom of the bin was an ugly green sweater. She held it up, smirking. She had never worn it, yet there it was. She tossed it into the donation bag.

Two months later, a man walked in wearing that very same green sweater at a local coffee shop. He looked happy—like the sweater was his favorite thing. Bella could not help herself. She approached him and said, "I used to own that sweater!" The man grinned. "Really? My sister gave it to me. She found it at a thrift store. It is my lucky sweater—I wore it to my job interview last week and got the job!" Bella laughed. Decluttering that sweater had not just cleared space; it had unknowingly brought someone else joy.

The Cluttered Life: Why We Feel Overwhelmed & the Promise of Less: Serenity, Joy, and Freedom are within reach by activating the 15 mins!

Wit for Chapter Introductions

1. Procrastination:
"If procrastination were an Olympic sport, I'd write this from a gold-medal podium. But since it's not, let's figure out why your junk drawer is now a junk closet"

2. On Decluttering Missteps:
"Remember when you donated your coffee maker... and then realized it was the only thing keeping you human before 9 a.m.? Let's avoid that level of chaos."

3. On ADHD Brain Logic:
"Somehow, in the ADHD brain, a pile of papers says 'organized,' but a labeled folder screams 'Where's the fun in that?' It's time to rewrite that narrative.

4. On Deciding What to Keep:
"If you haven't used it in the last 12 months, it's time to say goodbye. Exceptions: passports, your favorite sweater, and maybe that one Tupperware lid that still gives you hope.

5. On Sentimental Items:
"Just because Aunt Anne gave you a lamp shaped like a duck doesn't mean you must keep it. Love Aunt Anne, not her questionable taste in decor."

6. On buying Multiples:
"Unless you're hosting the Great Toaster Games, you don't need three toasters. Pick the least likely to set off your smoke alarm."

7. On Staying Motivated:
"Clutter didn't accumulate instantly, and it won't vanish instantly either... unless you hire a magician. If so, share their contact."

On Progress:

"Tossed out a pair of holey socks today? Congrats, you're winning at life."

8. Wit for ADHD-Specific Challenges

On Impulse Buying:
"The ADHD impulse-buying logic: 'This organizer will save my life!' Spoiler: it's now part of the clutter. Let's fix that."

9. On Time Blindness:
"When you think, 'This will only take five minutes,' multiply that by three and add a snack break for good measure."

Your Review is very much Welcome!
Please consider leaving a review on Amazon to assist others in making an informed decision about buying this book. You may open the link below or scan the QR code provided. Amazon Review Link

https://amazon.com/review/ dp/9798312176513 for the hardback!

TESS.
R   Do Check out my author Page on Amazon.com at
https://amazon.com/author/myworkingmemoryiscrap

CHAPTER 14 CLEANING HACKS!

Kitchen Cleaning Hacks

1. Steam Clean the Microwave:
Fill a microwave-safe bowl with water and a splash of vinegar. Microwave for 5 minutes, then leave to soak in and soften those stuck-on bits of food! Then, you wipe away loosened grime effortlessly with a cloth.

2. Grease-Proof your Cabinet Doors:
Apply a thin layer of dish soap and baking soda paste with a sponge. Wipe clean for grease-free surfaces

3. Shine Stainless Steel Appliances:
Use a dab of olive oil or vinegar on a microfiber cloth to remove smudges and make them sparkle.

4. Deodorize the Garbage Disposal:
Toss in a handful of ice cubes, a few lemon peels, and a pinch of baking soda. Run the disposal with ice cold water for a fresh-smelling sink.

Bathroom Cleaning Hacks

5. Clean Shower Heads with Vinegar:
Tie a plastic bag filled with vinegar around the showerhead and let it soak overnight to remove mineral deposits.

6. Fog-Free Mirrors:
Rub a small amount of shaving cream on the mirror and wipe it off. This prevents fogging after hot showers!

7. Grout Cleaner Made Easy:
Mix baking soda and hydrogen peroxide into a paste. Apply to grout lines, let it sit for 10 minutes, then scrub with an old toothbrush.

Living Room Cleaning Hacks

8. Dusting Ceiling Fans Without the Mess:
Slide an old pillowcase over the blades, then pull it back to catch all the dust.

9. Pet Hair Removal:
Use a damp rubber glove to swipe furniture and carpets. Pet hair clings instantly.

10. DIY Air Freshener:
Combine water, rubbing alcohol, and a few drops of your favorite essential oil in a spray bottle for a refreshing scent.

Bedroom Cleaning Hacks

11. Refresh Your Mattress:

Sprinkle baking soda over the mattress, let it sit for 30 minutes, and vacuum. Add essential oils for a fresh scent.

12. Repurpose Dryer Machine Sheets

Use dryer sheets to wipe baseboards; they repel dust and buff out the baseboards and skirt boards. And this helps keep them clean for longer.

13. Vacuum Cleaner Deodorizer:

Sprinkle baking soda mixed with a few drops of essential oil on carpets before vacuuming to freshen the room.

14. Windows Streak-Free:

Clean windows with a mix of water, vinegar, and a drop of dish soap. Wipe with crumpled Newspaper for a streak-free shine.

15. Multi-Purpose Cleaning Solution:

Mix equal parts vinegar and water with a few drops of lemon oil. Use counters, glass, and floors for all-natural cleaning.

The "How to" Clean Methods!

Step 1: Cut the clutter and do the dishes.

Things must be orderly to get deep clean going, so first, do away with the clutter. Put everything that does not belong in the kitchen in a box or bag and put it in another room. (You can deal with this later!) Then, put everything that does belong in the kitchen in its place, including all the dirty dishes in the sink.

Gather dirty dishcloths, aprons, kitchen towels, and other microfiber cloths for cleaning the kitchen and home. Put on a load of laundry—do not mix floor rugs with towels. Then, clean those dishes!

You cannot thoroughly clean if you cannot use the sink, so wash, dry, and put away all the dishes. If you have a dishwasher, fill it and move on to the next step while it runs.

Step 2: Dust from top to bottom

The right way to dust any room is top to bottom unless you want dust to fall from high above, float down, and land all over everything you dusted below.

Up high: Dust the light fixtures, cupboard tops, shelves, and fridge's top.

In the middle: Dust windows and sills, tables, shelves, and the like.

Dust the skirting boards/ baseboards, then sweep or dust mop the floor to remove the worst accumulated debris from the floor, so you do not walk it everywhere while you are cleaning.

Follow up with a damp microfiber cloth to remove stuck-on grease and grime from those surfaces. Why microfiber, you ask? It removes most dirt, grease, grime, and bacteria from the surface with zero cleaners needed. Always Buy the absolute best microfiber cloths and dusters.

Step 3: Clean small appliances

If your kitchen is overrun with small appliances, cleaning them alone can be lengthy. If your appliances are stainless steel, use olive oil or baby oil to enhance the shine after washing them. Here is a quick rundown on how to clean your trusty food Appliances.

The microwave

Place a bowl of water and a few drops of vinegar in the microwave and run it on high for 3-5 minutes. Leave the door closed for an hour, then open it up and wipe the loose, greasy deposits right up.

The coffee pot

Use the auto-clean button to clean the coffee maker with a 1:1 vinegar-to-water ratio. If there is no auto-cleaning, brew a couple of pots with a 1:1 vinegar-to-water ratio, scrub the basket, and clean the pot.

The toaster oven

To clean the toaster oven, sift or vacuum the burnt bits from the bottom. Wipe the inside with a damp microfiber cloth. Do not touch the heating elements, which are easily damaged.

The juicer

Add mild dish soap to a sink filled with warm water to clean your juicer. Disassemble the juicer, soak the components for 10 minutes, then wash and dry thoroughly.

The Instant One pot

Clean your instant pot by disassembling and soaking the pieces in soapy water. Wipe down the base and inside with a damp microfiber cloth. Wash and dry the pieces, then reassemble.

The air fryer

Disassemble your fryer and soak the pieces. Use a non-abrasive sponge to remove stuck-on food. Clean the air fryer base with a damp microfiber cloth, wash the parts, and reassemble.

Step 4: Clean the countertops, cupboards, and pantry.

Remove all items and wipe them down with an all-purpose cleaner to clean the countertops. Before you put each item back in its spot, wipe it down with a warm, damp microfiber cloth.

To clean the kitchen cabinets, remove the contents and throw out expired items as you go. Clean the inside of the cabinet with an all-purpose cleaner, then wipe down and replace the items that go back in.

To clean the pantry, remove all items, throw out expired items, put them onto your composting, or recycle as-you-go items as appropriate. Wipe down the shelves, sweep and mop the floor, and replace everything after wiping down each item.

Whether you have wood, granite, tile, or quartz countertops, you'll find a natural countertop-cleaning product.

Step 5: Clean the cooker.

The stovetop

To clean the stove burners and metal grills on a gas stove, soak them in lukewarm water and add a squirt of dish soap. For electric stovetop burners, gently spot-clean dirty areas with soap and a microfiber cloth, avoiding the connection points. To clean a glass stovetop, wipe it thoroughly with a microfiber cloth and water or vinegar, then go over it with a microfiber glass-cleaning cloth.

The oven

Following the helpful, step-by-step oven-cleaning guide, mix half a cup of baking soda with 2 to 3 tablespoons of water to create a paste. Use the paste and a gentle scrub brush to scour the oven interior, avoiding elements. Let the paste sit overnight, then use a microfiber cloth, water, and distilled white vinegar to remove the baking soda and give it a final shine.

Step 6: Clean the sink.

Your sink gets dirty quickly, but the rubbish disposal and drain get slimy, grimy, and moldy overnight.

Once again, use baking soda, water paste, and a sponge or microfiber cloth to wipe down the entire sink basin. Then, use an old toothbrush coated in the paste to scrub as much of the drain area as possible. Spray distilled white vinegar over the baking soda, which will fizz up and loosen any stubborn gunk. Let it sit for a few minutes, scrub, then rinse with water, and hey presto! You have a clean sink!

To naturally clean your drain, pour a half-cup of baking soda and a half-cup of vinegar. Plug the drain and leave it for an hour. Then, pull the plug and pour a pot of boiling water down the drain.

Step 7: Clean out the fridge.

Kitchen cleaning tasks: Clean out the fridge. This should be carried out the day before your garbage is collected.

Start by emptying everything in your fridge. Throw out or compost anything that looks like a failed or expired lab experiment. Put the edible contents on your now-empty countertops.

Pull out the removable trays, drawers, and shelves and soak them in warm, soapy water.

Use a hot, damp microfiber cloth to clean the inside of the fridge and door. While they dry, air-dry, wash the shelves and drawers in hot, soapy water, rinse thoroughly, dry, and replace.

Rinse and recycle the containers you emptied and wipe down the fridge's exterior.

Step 8: Empty the rubbish and clean the bin.

Take out the rubbish and turn the whole bin upside down over the outdoor bin to empty any wayward rubbish. If it's horrid inside, hose it out—or give it a hot shower—while scrubbing it with a heavy-duty brush.

If it's not that bad, use an all-purpose cleaner to wipe down the bin's interior and exterior—get the lid, hinges, and foot pedal—then put in a new eco-friendly liner, and your rubbish bin will no longer stink.

Step 9: Clean the floor.
It's time to vacuum thoroughly. Run the hose along the skirting boards /baseboards, behind the fridge, under shelves and cupboards, and in all the cracks and crevices in your kitchen.

Give the floor a good mopping with the appropriate cleaner for your floor type, or use a steam cleaner if you have one to clean the floors.

Step 10:
Update or freshen your curtains and pillow covers and take a well-deserved break/Rest as you have worked hard to clean your kitchen. Admire your fine work!

Other Methods to Try:

1. Clean as you go.
Cleaning as you go is one of the secrets to staying on top of chores, and it is a top tip. "Cleaning as you go

when cooking. It is Life changing." There is much advice to be had on completing small cleaning tasks while waiting for something else, like pasta boiling on the stove or leftovers warming up in the microwave. You could wipe down a cupboard door, tidy a drawer, or remove any leftovers in the fridge.

2. My Best Cleaning Tip!

I learned from my mom to use a dirty hand towel to wipe down the bathroom basin and the back of the toilet before you toss it into the laundry basket. I wash hand towels frequently, so those surfaces stay tidy. I do that with my face wipes, too. After I wiped and washed my face, I wiped down the surfaces. I clean my bathroom as I go to keep it looking clean to the casual observer, and it gets a deep clean once weekly.

3. Use a Daily Shower Cleaner

Try to keep your shower glass from getting a buildup of minerals!

Like many people, I use a daily shower cleaner after every shower to keep my glass doors free of soap scum and hard water build up. I also take the extra step of using a squeegee to prevent excess stains.

4. Keep on Top of washing Dishes

Simple cleaning tasks like washing dishes can be a mindful act of self-care, but they can also snowball into a massive list of things to do that require the lion's share of a weekend to feel like your home is back in hand. Not every cleaning strategy will work for you, but now and again, one stumble on a tip or habit so good, you think, "I can't believe others don't do this!"

5. Clean the fridge the night before the garbage is collected.

I clean the fridge every time the trash is collected, whether weekly or fortnightly. If the bins must be put out incredibly early in the morning, I dump my old food the night before. We always have room in the fridge, and when leaving food in the bin, we can wait until the bins are collected. This helps to prevent the trash from getting too smelly too quickly!

6."Do Not Put anything down, put it Away."

This simple strategy, known as the **OHIO** method (only handle it once), avoids clutter build-up and helps break habits like leaving stuff out.

7. Sort silverware/cutlery before loading the dishwasher.

If you want to reduce the time it takes to unpack the dishwasher, "sorting the silverware as you put it in the dishwasher makes it way easier to unload." This tip is divisive—some manufacturers recommend sorting cutlery, while others advise against it due to "spooning," where silverware sticks together and isn't washed correctly.

8. Leave some trash bags at the bottom of the rubbish bins!

Few things are more frustrating than finding the trash/rubbish/garbage can empty without a new bag. Stash a few empty ones at the bottom of your trash bin to make replacing the bag less hassle. "Next time the bag gets full, there's a new one. There's no need to have one to take out the full one."

9. Clean your cleaning tools.

If you're diligent about busting dust but forget that your cleaning tools also need maintenance, "Occasionally deep clean the vacuum, especially if you have long-haired people in the household." Tip for washable vacuum filters: Stock up extras to pop in a replacement while waiting for the washed one to dry.

10. Never leave a room empty-handed.

Never exit a room without picking up something for another room. "If I'm leaving the living room to go into the kitchen, I look around to see if any dishes or anything else needs to be returned to the kitchen. When I leave my bedroom to go to the bathroom, I look around to see if I brought any lotions or makeup out that needs to go back." Pair this with the one-touch rule for the ultimate anti-clutter combo.

11. Clean the shower.

Turn it into a clean-as-you-go task. "I keep one of those shower scrub sponges in the shower and clean the glass while my conditioner soaks in. The secret to this hack is Keeping a scrub sponge in the bathroom close to the shower. Then, you can clean the glass as you wait for the two minutes needed for your hair conditioner to take effect!

12. Microwave

Boil a small bowl of water in the microwave before cleaning it.

Food splatters inside a microwave can be ultra-hard to budge — making this tip especially Useful. "To clean your microwave, put a bowl of water in for three to five minutes, let it sit a few more after it's done, and it makes everything come off so much easier," This is especially effective if you add vinegar to the water.

13. Vacuum

Before cleaning the bathroom.

Chasing a couple of elusive hairs all over a toilet base is not your idea of an enjoyable time. Save yourself this infuriating dynamic by vacuuming hair strands and dust particles before wiping, scrubbing, or sanitizing tasks. Yes, it is common sense to vacuum before mopping, but vacuum not only the floor but also the "back of the toilet, counters, tub, and shower." That way, you can avoid having to wipe hair and wet dust back and forth, shifting it from one location to another!

14. Clean your bathroom

Feel free to customize your cleaning routine to suit your needs and preferences. You can either follow the suggested order or focus on a specific area that needs more attention. The choice is entirely yours. You can even spread out the tasks over a few days or weeks. Here are some places you should consider.

Take everything out of your bathroom — and clean those things.

This includes things inside the shower or tub (shower products like shampoo, conditioner, soap, etc., and a shower caddy), outside it (like the curtain, liner, and items on your shelves and counters), and on the floor (such as the bathmat, trash can, toilet cleaner, and plunger). Throw anything that can be machine-washed into the washer, then wipe down all your products and items.

Focus on the shower or tub.

You can work from top to bottom or pick what you want to work on and skip the rest.

Clean the shower head. For quick cleaning, you could wipe it down with some all-purpose cleaner. But, for something more profound, you should consider soaking it in a bag of vinegar to remove buildup.

Scrub your shower or tub using a dedicated shower cleaner or plain dish soap with a scrub brush /sponge to clean from top to bottom. You may need to let your cleaner sit to let it work its magic—just be sure to check the instructions and properly ventilate the room. Do not forget to scrub the shower door and see if soap or mineral deposits are built up.

Clean the grout, carefully looking at any dingy or moldy areas. Hydrogen peroxide and baking soda are great combos for fighting stubborn grout grime.

Now that you've scrubbed everything in the bathroom spray it with water.

Clean the toilet pan.

Start by cleaning inside the toilet and letting the cleaner work its magic. Then, scrub all around the bathroom — including the back and the walls! If you can, remove the seat to clean the hinges. When you are all done, flush the toilet.

Repurpose Dryer Sheets

Cleaning your house does not require spending much money on expensive cleaning products. Many items you usually throw away around your home can help clean tasks. When combined with water, vinegar, and a little dish soap, then Hey, Presto!

Take dryer sheets, for instance. Instead of throwing them out once you unload the laundry, save them for other tasks around the home. They can help buff out smudges on windows or mirrors, wipe down scuffed skirting boards or baseboards, and more.

Do not forget that dryer sheets can also freshen up items. Keep a dryer sheet in your linen closet or t-shirt drawer. I also use scented candles in my bed linen closet and cupboards. This way, they will not get a musty smell and can smell pleasant, like the candle scent!

Cleaning the Blinds

Like air vents, blinds are another household item that is easy to forget and yet difficult to clean.

Cleaning blinds doesn't have to be a daunting task. You can easily do it with just a few household items. I usually use wet wipes or a simple solution of warm water, dish soap, and a splash of vinegar. Then, I put an old sock over my hand, dampen it with water, and run it over the blinds. It's that simple!

Tip: Use Vinegar with added Baking Soda if you need it to be abrasive to Clean Your Faucets/Taps. Vinegar and baking Soda are beneficial for many cleaning tasks around the house. Vinegar's acidic nature makes it a great disinfectant, while baking soda's alkaline nature makes it an effective cleaner and deodorizer. Combined, they create a powerful cleaning solution that can tackle tough stains and grime.

No More Smelly Upholstered Furniture

Upholstered furniture can be hard to clean. You cannot take the fabric off your couch and throw it in the washing machine. Over time, odors from sweat, skin, and pets can make your couch smell musty.

Once again, baking soda can help eliminate odors. Sprinkle baking soda on your furniture and let it sit for at least twenty minutes. Then, vacuum it up and enjoy the fresh new scent.

To Unclog Your Sink /Toilet Pan

If your sink drains slowly, don't buy chemicals to unclog the drains. Not only are they expensive, but they can corrode your pipes over time.

Instead, combine water, vinegar, and baking soda to do the job.

Start by pouring a pot of boiling water down the drain. Then, pour baking soda and a solution of equal parts hot water and vinegar.

If you've ever made a volcano in science class, you know what happens when you mix vinegar and baking soda. Apparently, you can use Mentos! The bubbling reaction will help break up the buildup in your drain.

Rest assured; this method is effective. If the drain doesn't flow, repeat the process a few times. But with some patience, your sink/basin or toilet pan will run smoothly again.

Putting House Cleaning Hacks to Work

Now that you've learned about the importance of spring cleaning and how to draft a plan of action let's dive into some house cleaning hacks that will make your cleaning tasks more efficient and effective. With these hacks, you'll soon see better results from your cleaning time. That said, no matter how many tips and tricks you learn, keeping up with all the cleaning is still time-consuming. If you need some extra help to get your house sparkling

Call your cleaners in!

Spring is a time to start fresh, and this is especially true for your home.

It's time to clean out the cobwebs and dust bunnies, scrub down walls and floors, and eliminate the clutter gathering all winter.

This will work just as well for your spring and winter checklists when you come to clean the house ready for Winter and Christmas festivities! A spring checklist may include tasks like deep cleaning, decluttering, and organizing, while a winter checklist may focus on preparing the house for the holidays and colder weather.

Whether you're doing it yourself or hiring a professional Spring-Cleaning service, follow these deep-cleaning tips and tricks to help ensure that this spring clean goes off without a hitch.

1. Draw Up A PLAN OF ACTION

Kick off your spring cleaning by getting organized.

What areas within your home need the most attention?

What spots do you skip when you quickly clean up at the end of a long day?

Those places need a little more attention during your deep-cleaning session.

During this planning stage, you must have all the necessary cleaning supplies, so you do not need to stop mid-cleaning to get extra reinforcements.

Create a plan for each room.

Look at your appliances, floor, counters, and cabinets— dust around the TV in the living room. Do not forget to go outside your house as well. Here is an example of a spring-cleaning checklist for outdoor areas: Get yourself a quality home maintenance guide!

2. External Areas:

Clean and/or repair gutters

Clean light fixtures

Clean outdoor furniture

Clean sliding door tracks

Clean and organize the garage.

Mow the lawn and plant fresh flowers.

Creating a separate spring-cleaning checklist for each area of your home can keep you organized. That way, you will not have to worry about missing anything once you start getting busy. A schedule can also help you break different rooms up. Instead of exhausting yourself, schedule a break.

3. Start Decluttering

Clutter can impact your stress level and make cleaning seem daunting.

Look around. Which area seems like the most enormous mess? Start there!

Tackling the expensive items first can make the rest of your household seem more straightforward.

First things first: get organized. Clean through wardrobes and closets, fold the laundry, and manage your desk. Getting rid of clutter first can give you the space you need to clean.

Once you start decluttering and organizing, you will feel your stress melting!

4. Start from the top and work your way down.

Start from the ceiling and work your way down. To optimize your time, vacuum cobwebs and dust from ceilings and fans before the floors.

5. Vacuum.

Choosing the right vacuum can benefit your entire spring-cleaning checklist. A high-quality HEPA vacuum will catch even the smallest dust particles. As part of your spring-cleaning apparatus, try to get a HEPA vacuum to remove dirt, dust, and other allergens from your home.

If you want a new vacuum, look for one with attachments and crevice tools. Is it a HEPA vacuum? Purchase the best quality you can afford. If it is HEPA, does it pick up the smallest dust particles?

Consider purchasing a quality steam cleaner. They are great for bathrooms, kitchen appliances, floors, and sofa cushions. If it comes with attachments, it is all the better.

6. To the Windows and the Walls

Dust does not discriminate. It sits on surfaces other than countertops and floors. Remember to add windows and walls to your spring-cleaning checklist, too.

Start from the top of your blinds and walls and work your way down. Once you are done inside, head outside to remove and clean your window screens.

7. Attack the Trouble Areas First.

The dust is in the details! Dust and dirt can collect everywhere, so you need to clean everywhere.

Tackling these items can ensure thorough, deep cleanliness.

Air It Out and Open Doors and windows so fresh air can flow through your home.

Your filters are essential to improving the air quality within your home. Switching to fresh filters can also ensure your AC runs optimally.

8. Avoid Allergy Attacks
To protect family members from allergy attacks, Dust

Check product labels.

Wear gloves, masks, and protective clothing while you clean.

Consider buying an air purifier.

You'll kick dust into the air as you complete your spring-cleaning list. An air purifier can remove dust, allergens, and odors from the air to prepare everyone for the allergy season.

9. Update Soft Furnishings:
Such as curtains, blinds, cushions, and so on. Think about adding new pillows, towels, and bedding to your home. If your curtains are dark, switch to sheer. A few minor changes can make a significant difference as spring rolls in. Your home will need another spring clean at the end of summer, but this time for the winter and/or Christmas festivities.

10. DOGS AND PETS IN GENERAL

Do dogs not sweat? I did not know that, at least, I don't remember! And even more importantly, how do they stink up your house so badly?

Oils on their skin, bacteria in their ears, scents from their anal gland, and leftovers in their teeth all contribute to the distinct smell of your dog. These are factors that never go away, even with an occasional bath.

The question remains of how to get rid of dogs or other pet smells in your home, especially when your pets smell well!

To eliminate pet smell in your house, start with regular cleaning to keep the smell to a minimum. You can also hire a local house cleaning service to come in and deep clean everything, including floors, walls, and furniture, to make your home sparkling and shiny again.

If you don't want to spend money on deep-cleaning services, try these tips to keep the pet smell to just the pet and not their sleeping area or other soft furnishings!

1. Start With a Bath

Beginning with the source of the smell, brush your pet to remove loose hair. You can bathe a dog, and I have heard of some cats allowing their owners to wash their cats! I am not joking, but I have never had a feline that enjoyed me turning the shower on for them. This will give you a fresh start before cleaning. If it is a nice day, put your pet outside to keep the pet smell from further affecting your home.

Your dog can dry and sanitize in the sun while you get to work. While your dog or other pet is outside dry playing in the mud, I have no doubt! At least they're not leaving filthy, dirty footprints. You can start by cleaning its things, such as your nice, clean bed sheets or other soft furnishings that have been slept on!

2. Gather Your Dog's items: his bed and such.

If you want to eliminate dog odor, it's time to disinfect everything your dog loves. Bowls, toys, blankets, and leashes can be cleaned to remove bacteria and dander. By removing these items first, you can ensure that more odors do not get released into the air while cleaning everything else.

You can throw fabrics in the washer and clean complex objects like bowls with a non-toxic cleaner. Once everything is clean, set it outside to free up some space for more cleaning.

3. Get Washing

Fabrics hold smells more than anything. Grab any washable and detachable fabric, such as couch covers, pillowcases, curtains, sheets, and clothes. Once your dog's or other pets' belongings are collected, toss them in the washer.

4. Sweep the Floors

The most effective way to get rid of dog odor in your house begins with hair. Hair can carry dander, dirt, and oils that spread throughout your home.

So, before you go crazy with the vacuum cleaner, get excess hair up with a broom. This will limit the times you need to empty your vacuum and keep large clumps of hair from blowing around. Sometimes, vacuuming can miss the messiest spots and blow them under the furniture. Sweeping is much more efficient for very hairy dogs.

5. Get Out the Mop

Mopping gets even more dirt and leftover hair. Hard surfaces may contain invisible paw prints and grime from your dog's romp in the park. Mopping also disinfects to eliminate bacteria-causing smells. Open the windows after you mop to get a fresh flow of air circulating in your home and release the odors.

6. Vacuum Time

Now that the floors are clean, how do you get the dog smell out of the carpet? A good vacuum cleaner is necessary when you have a pet (and carpet).

Ensure the suction is unclogged, the container is empty, and the bristles are on the lowest setting.

Go over areas where the dog tends to sleep and play several times. And don't forget to see the furniture, over shelves, and on top of lampshades. You can use an attachment to vacuum furniture that cannot be washed.

7. Use an Air Purifier

Sometimes, bacteria and unpleasant odors linger in the air. Get a high-quality air purifier.

A high-quality purifier pulls dander and hair directly from the air before it latches onto floors and furniture. It's especially great if you or your friends and family have dog allergies. An alternative to air purifiers is house plants that naturally filter the air.

8. Do a Black Light Test

When your pet is home alone, there is no telling when and where they may have used your carpet for a bathroom or waste bin. A black-light can show trouble areas that may need professional cleaning. Steam cleaning these areas can get urine or any throw-up that has set into the fibers of carpets and rugs.

You can even check the furniture to see how to get rid of the dog smell. Couches can also be steam cleaned.

9. Paint with Odor Sealer

An odor-sealing paint will at least remove the bad smells.

10. Lastly, add Some Fragrance to your lovely clean areas!

AMAZON REVIEW

Please open the link, which will direct you to my Amazon review page. I hope this process works smoothly for you.

https://www/amazon.com/review/97983099 93833 or 9798312176513

If that does not work, scan the QR code.

Please scan the QR Code to be directed to the review page on Amazon. Your feedback is valuable as it assists other potential buyers and allows for updates if necessary.

Thank you, Tess R.

Cleaning
CHECKLIST

DAILY

- [ ] Make Bed
- [ ] Wash Dishes
- [ ] Wipe Kitchen Table
- [ ] Do Laundry
- [ ] Sweep Kitchen Floors
- [ ] Clean Bathroom
- [ ] Brush Shower Walls
- [ ] Sanitize Kitchen & Bathroom

WEEKLY

- [ ] Clean Mirrors
- [ ] Clean Windows
- [ ] Dust Furnitures
- [ ] Change Beddings
- [ ] Do Laundry
- [ ] Garbage Disposal
- [ ] Clean Oven/Microwave
- [ ] Mop floors

MONTHLY

- [ ] Clean Storages
- [ ] Clean Fridge
- [ ] Clean Rooms
- [ ] Change Beddings
- [ ] Wipe Kitchen Cabinets
- [ ] Scrub Stove & Burners
- [ ] Declutter Cabinets
- [ ] Vacuum upholstery

YEARLY

- [ ] Empty Pantry
- [ ] Empty Shelves
- [ ] Deep clean carpets
- [ ] Dust lampshades
- [ ] Deep Clean Windows
- [ ] Clear out gutters
- [ ] Deep Clean upholstery
- [ ] Aircon Cleaning

https://advancedpsychiatryassociates.com/res ources/blog/adhd-clutter-management-guide

Understanding Sensory Overload in Autism: Navigating the World of Overwhelming Stimuli **https://www.udontseemautistic.com/post/unde rstanding-sensory-overload-in-autism-navigating-the-world-of-overwhelming-stimuli**

Understanding ADHD Clutter Anxiety: Causes, Overcoming Decision Fatigue in ADHD **https://www.psychologytoday.com/us/blog/ch anging-the-narrative-on-adhd/202405/overcoming-decision-fatigue-in-adhd**

How to Get Rid of Stuff You No Longer Use or Need https://www.additudemag.com/emotional-attachment-letting-go-of-stuff/

The S.M.A.R.T Plan for Decluttering Success
https://medium.com/@declutterbuzz/the-s-m-a-r-t-plan-for-decluttering-success-62e066969d37

ADHD Apps: Mobile Resources for ADD Minds
https://www.additudemag.com/mobile-apps-for-adhd-minds/

Using a Home Inventory to Declutter (with printable checklist)

https://www.ithinkwecouldbefriends.com/2021/06/29/home-inventory/r/declutter

https://www.reddit.com/r/declutter/

How to Declutter: Tips When You Have ADHD
https://psychcentral.com/adhd/ways-to-clear-out-clutter-when-you-have-adhd

How to Declutter Your Home in 15 Minutes a Day
https://medium.com/expurgo/declutter-your-
home-in-15-minutes-a-day-a3688396f74d

How to Focus Better with ADHD: 12 Ways - Mind Health Group
https://www.mindhealthgroup.com/blog/ways-to-focus-better-with-

adhd/#:~:text=Chunk%20Your%20Tasks,
do%20list%20and%20keep%20focused.

The Many Mental Benefits of Decluttering
https://www.psychologytoday.com/us/blog/the
-

resilient-brain/202302/the-many-mental-benefits-of-
decluttering

How to Declutter: 7 Tips for ADHD Adults
https://www.additudemag.com/slideshows/ho
w-

to-declutter-adhd/

The Impact of Minimalism on Mental Health Momo
Lifestyle_____**https://momo-**
lifestyle.com/blogs/better-life-tips/the-impact-
of-minimalism-on-mental-

health#:
~:text=By%20eliminating%20unnecessary%20items%2
0and,
quality%2C%20and%20reduced%20anxiety%20levels.

Kitchen Organization for Efficient Cooking
https://www.thescramble.com/organizing-
stocking-kitchen/kitchen-organization-for-
efficient-

cooking/?srsltid=AfmBOopVT4Naj-
rpA2jiSYSdXBGwOVvCTUyW0LzjBkOCMxCMay7PxJ9

Office ergonomics: Your how-to guide - Mayo Clinic
https://www.mayoclinic.org/healthy-
lifestyle/adult-health/in-depth/office-
ergonomics/art-
20046169#:~:text=You%20may%20be%20able

%20to,posture%20all%20make%20a%20differe
nce.

How to Declutter: Tips When You Have ADHD
**https://psychcentral.com/adhd/ways-to-clear-
out-clutter-when-you-have-adhd**

Letting Go: How to Get Rid of Emotional Attachments
to Items **https://www.cubesmart.com/blog/your-
space/letting-go-how-to-get-rid-of-emotional-**

attachments-to-items/

Author Margareta Magnussen coined the term
'Swedish death cleaning' in her 2018 book, *'The Gentle
Art of Swedish Death Cleaning: How to Free Yourself
and Your Family from a Lifetime of Clutter.'*

15 Science-Backed Benefits of Minimalism
**https://modernminimalism.com/science-
backed-benefits-of-
minimalism/#:~:text=Minimalism%20can%20h
ave%20substantial%20mental,helping%20kee
p%20cortisol%**

20levels%20balanced.

How to Declutter & Sort Sentimental Items (Without
Guilt)
**https://www.apartmenttherapy.com/declutter-
sentimental-items-37422075**

Tips for Daily Decluttering for ADHD Adults
https://www.additudemag.com/neat-tricks-tips-for-daily-decluttering/

How Do I Get Motivated to Clean When I Have ADHD?
https://www.additudemag.com/how-do-i-get-motivated-to-clean-adhd/#:~:text=Plus%2C%20hard%20work%20goes%20faster,ADHD%20brain%20moving%20and%20motivated.

&text=Just%20remember%20that%20trying%20to, you%20feeling%20overwhelmed%20and%20frustrated.

Decision Fatigue: 6 Ways to Defog Your Brain
https://www.betterup.com/blog/decision-fatigue

Using Creative Visualization to Declutter Your Life and
...   **https://reawakenyourbrilliance.com/using-creative-visualization-to-declutter-your-life/**

Digital Detox: Reclaiming Your Mental Health from Social   ...
https://apogeebehavioralmedicine.com/blog/digital-detox-reclaiming-your-mental-health-from-social-media/

Digital Organization and ADHD: Why It Matters
https://www.upskillspecialists.com/post/digital-organization-and-

adhd#:
~:text=For%20individuals%20with%20ADHD%2C
%20digital,
can%20have%20the%20opposite%20effect.

The best document management software in 2024

https://zapier.com/blog/best-document-management-software/

How to Manage Social Media Notifications
Effectively - LinkedIn
Https://www.llnkedln.com/advlce/0/what-most-effective-ways-manage-social-media-notifications-lwsfc

Minimalism and ADHD (Attention Deficit
Hyperactivity ...
https://balancethroughsimplicity.com/minimalism-and-adhd/

Mindfulness Decluttering Techniques
https://www.trimbox.io/blog/mindfulness-decluttering-techniques

Creating Tranquil Balance: A Guide to Feng Shui Your
Home
https://www.studiojeandre.com/post/feng-shui-your-home

Balance Minimalism with everyday life - Declutter Your
Life
https://declutteryourlife.co.uk/minimalism/finding-harmony-balance-minimalism-with-the-practicality-of-everyday-life/

Decluttering with ADHD: Practical Tips for Simplifying **https://www.happysimplemom.com/declutterin g-with-adhd/**

Organizing Shared Spaces - The Byzantine Life - Plus Video! **https://thebyzantinelife.com/organizing-shared-spaces/**

Understanding Disposophobic (AKA The Fear of Throwing Things Away). **https://dnqsolutions.medium.com/understandi ng-disposaphobia-aka-the-fear-of-throwing-things-away-a37543f9fadd**

6 Ways to Create Decluttering Habits That Stick **https://www.pacificprime.lat/blog/6-ways-to-create-decluttering-habits-that-stick/**

Let's Make Things Visual: Supporting Children with ADHD ... **https://neilsonmahoneycoaching.com/lets-make-things-visual/**

A Game You Can Win: Using Gamification in Your ... **https://www.clutterfairyhouston.com/a-game-you-can-win-using-gamification-in-your-organizing-process/**

Online ADHD Management Tools for Adults - ADDA **https://add.org/adhd-tools-for-adults/**

Visual Reminders for ADHD: Enhance Productivity
https://neurolaunch.com/visual-reminders-for-adhd/

ADHD and Clutter: Effective Decluttering Techniques
https://declutterhub.com/declutter-adhd/

https://www.additudemag.com/tag/adhd-diagnosis-decisions-adults/?ecd=wnl_adhd_vol6_cons_path_diagad&goal=0_4a4ec7e6d0-765d34ff8d-[LIST_EMAIL_ID]

Why is it important to declutter? How can it benefit your   ...
https://www.foresthomesstore.com/blogs/decor-for-wellbeing/why-is-it-important-to-declutter-how-can-it-benefit-your-mental-health-and-others-wellbeing

Success   Stories   -   Clutter   Clearing
https://www.clutterclearing.net/success-stories/.

10 Strategies for Cultivating Community Accountability
https://transformharm.org/ca_resource/10-strategies-for-cultivating-community-accountability/

My ADHD Clutter Story by Melanie
https://caddac.ca/my-adhd-clutter-story-by-melanie/

The Importance of Routine for Adults with ADHD
https://www.psychiatrynyc.com/blog/the-importance-of-routine-for-adults-with-adhd/

15 Science-Backed Benefits of Minimalism
https://modernminimalism.com/science-backed-benefits-of-minimalism/

15 Super Helpful Decluttering Tips for Busy People
https://www.becomingminimalist.com/decluttering-tips-for-busy-people

Managing ADHD Hyperfocus and Turning Them to Our Advantage.
https://www.theminiadhdcoach.com/living-with-adhd/adhd-hyperfocus

https://www.webmd.com/add-adhd/rejection-sensitive-dysphoria

https://www.webmd.com/add-adhd/adhd-adults

https://www.digitaltrends.com/mobile/best-apps-for-limiting-your-screen-time/#dt-heading-digital-wellbeing

https://www.betterup.com/blog/how-to-hold-yourself-accountable

https://www.betterup.com/for-individuals/life-coaching

https://www.betterup.com/blog/how-to-hold-yourself-accountable

https://chadd.org/for-adults/diagnosis-of-adhd-in-adults/

"Validation of the dispositional adult hyperfocus questionnaire (AHQ-D) K. E. Hupfeld, J. B. Osborne, ...P." https://www.nature.com/articles/s41598024-70028 y#:~:text=Validation%20of%20the,%2C%20%E2%80%A6P.

https://www.goodreads.com/quotes/8760745-you-own-your-feelings-you-own-your-thoughts-you-

control#:~:text=You%20own%20your,of%2Dthe%2
Dmind

https://www.additudemag.com/wasting-time-adhd-
and-time-
perception/?ecd=wnl_additude_250128_cons_adhd
_adult&goal=0_d9446392d6-898ca046bc-327428745

Printed in Great Britain
by Amazon

59711779R00126